ACCOUNTING PRACTICES
FOR HOTELS, MOTELS,
AND RESTAURANTS

Bobbs-Merrill Educational Publishing

Hotel-Motel Management Series
Series Editor: DAVID HERTZSON

ACCOUNTING PRACTICES FOR HOTELS, MOTELS, AND RESTAURANTS
   by Paul Dittmer
DINING ROOM SERVICE
   by Lewis Lehrman
ELEMENTS OF FOOD PRODUCTION AND BAKING, SECOND EDITION
   by Joseph F. Vastano
FOOD AND BEVERAGE COST CONTROLS
   by Bruno Maizel
FOOD AND BEVERAGE PURCHASING
   by Bruno Maizel
FRONT OFFICE OPERATION
   by Joseph J. Haszonics
FUNCTIONAL HOUSEKEEPING IN HOTELS AND MOTELS
   by John T. Fales
HOSPITALITY INDUSTRY COOPERATIVE TRAINING
   by Seymour Hertzson
HOTEL-MOTEL MARKETING
   by David Hertzson
INTRODUCTION TO THE HOSPITALITY INDUSTRY
   by Nathan Kalt
LEGAL ASPECTS OF HOTEL, MOTEL, AND RESTAURANT OPERATION
   by Nathan Kalt
MANAGEMENT OF HOSPITALITY OPERATIONS
   by Bruce H. Axler
MENU PLANNING AND FOODS MERCHANDISING
   by Restaurant Business, Inc.
PERSONNEL MANAGEMENT AND HUMAN RELATIONS
   by John R. Zabka
SANITATION, SAFETY, AND MAINTENANCE MANAGEMENT
   by Bruce Axler

ACCOUNTING PRACTICES FOR HOTELS, MOTELS, AND RESTAURANTS

Paul Dittmer

Hotel and Restaurant Management Department
New York City Community College

Bobbs-Merrill Educational Publishing
Indianapolis

The Bobbs-Merrill Company, Inc.
4300 West 62nd Street
Indianapolis, Indiana 46268

Library of Congress Catalog Card Number: 79-142507
ISBN 0-672-96062-1
First Edition
Sixth Printing—1978

Contents

Preface

Accounting Practices for Hotels, Motels, and Restaurants is written for students beginning their study of the hospitality industry and for those already in the field who want to increase their understanding of the accounting aspects of the industry. It is a beginning text, written in fundamental terms. The illustrations are simplified for easy understanding.

The author hopes that this text will serve as an adequate starting point for those students who wish to make accounting their specialty in the hospitality industry, and at the same time provide a sufficient background for those who will serve in some other capacity to understand the importance of the work of the accountant in a successful operation.

I would like to express my gratitude to the editors for their unremitting cooperation, and to my wife, Barbara, whose devotion and patience made my work a hundredfold easier.

1 | A Review of Basic Accounting Principles

Your work in basic accounting has been designed to acquaint you with those accounting principles and procedures applicable to all forms of business. These basic principles and procedures will not change in your study of hotel accounting. The process of journalizing, posting, obtaining a trial balance, and completing the accounting cycle will remain the same. However, a hotel is a very special business due to the many different departments within it, each performing a unique service for the customer. Consequently the columnar journals, the income statement, and other accounting records will look unlike those of any other business.

Let us begin the study of hotel accounting by reviewing the principles you have learned in your basic accounting course. Instead of dealing with a general store or a furniture store, you will be dealing with a hotel. In this way, you can reacquaint yourself with the basic material so important to an understanding of hotel accounting, and at the same time you will begin to use the language of hotels.

THE FUNDAMENTAL EQUATION

You will recall that the basic accounting relationship is

Assets = liabilities + capital

Assets are defined as something of value owned by a business. Liabilies are the creditors' claims upon the assets of the business. Capital is ıe ownership claim on the assets of the business.

1

The fundamental equation can be altered by

1. *Increasing or decreasing the owner's investment.* Roger Young, owner of Roger Young's Hotel, increases his investment in the hotel by $5,000. The amount of cash in the business (asset) is increased by $5,000, and Roger Young's capital account is also increased by $5,000.

2. *Exchanging one asset for another asset.* We purchase $400 worth of food for cash. The value of our food inventory is increased by $400, but the value of our cash account is decreased by $400. Note that the total value of our assets would not change. Our cash asset is decreased by exactly the same amount as our food asset is increased.

3. *Purchasing an asset on account.* We purchase $200 worth of housekeeping supplies and do not pay for them immediately. Our housekeeping supply inventory increases by $200 (asset), and our accounts payable (liability) also increases by $200. We have increased both sides of the fundamental equation by $200.

4. *Paying our debts.* We pay the housekeeping supply bill incurred above. Our liabilities and our assets decrease. Cash would decrease by $200, and accounts payable would also decrease by $200.

5. *Making a profit or loss.* There are two sets of changes that occur in the fundamental equation when a profit or loss is made: income is generated that will increase both assets and capital; and expenses will be created that will decrease assets and capital. We sell $100 worth of food for $400 in cash. Our cash account (asset) will increase by $400, and our capital will increase by $400. At the same time, our food inventory will decrease by $100, and our capital will decrease by $100. The net result is an increase in our capital of $300. The income account that increases capital is called food sales, and the expense account that decreases capital is called food expense.

Figure 1.1 shows the effect of the above transactions on the fundamental equation.

DEBITS AND CREDITS

The word "debit" simply means an entry to the *left-hand side* of a ledger account, and the word "credit" means an entry to the *right-hand side* of a ledger account. Debits and credits can increase or decrease

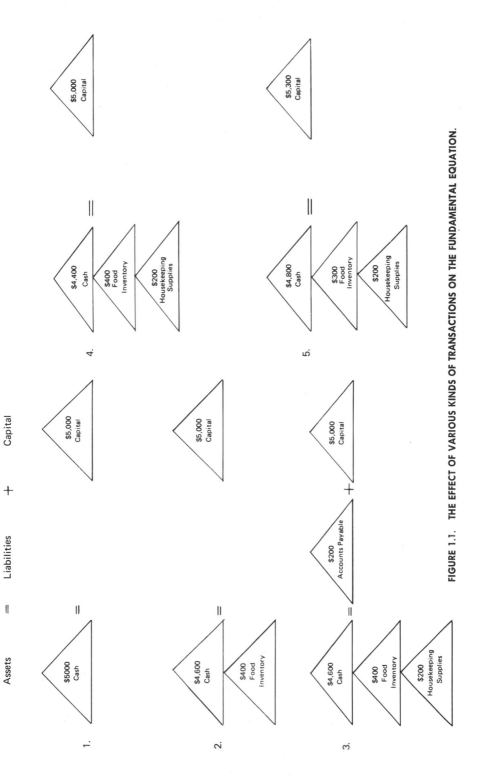

Assets = Liabilities + Capital

1. $5000 Cash = $5,000 Capital

2. $4,600 Cash + $400 Food Inventory = $5,000 Capital

3. $4,600 Cash + $400 Food Inventory + $200 Housekeeping Supplies = $200 Accounts Payable + $5,000 Capital

4. $4,400 Cash + $400 Food Inventory + $200 Housekeeping Supplies = $5,000 Capital

5. $4,800 Cash + $300 Food Inventory + $200 Housekeeping Supplies = $5,300 Capital

FIGURE 1.1. THE EFFECT OF VARIOUS KINDS OF TRANSACTIONS ON THE FUNDAMENTAL EQUATION.

accounts, depending upon which account we are talking about. The table below summarizes the rules you should follow:

Table 1.1. EFFECTS OF DEBITS AND CREDITS ON ACCOUNTS

Account	Debit	Credit
Assets	+	—
Liabilities	—	+
Capital	—	+
Income	—	+
Expenses	+	—

Thus, if we want to show an increase in our cash account, we would debit it because it is an asset account. If we want to show an increase in the accounts payable account, we would credit it because it is a liability account. To show a decrease in our cash account we would credit it, and to show a decrease in our accounts payable account we would debit it. Since income increases our capital account, we will credit all income accounts to show increases, and since increased expenses decrease our capital account, we will debit expense accounts to show an increase in expenses. Some of the more common income accounts you will be using in hotel accounting are room sales, food sales, liquor sales, and telephone sales. Some of the more common expense accounts you will be using are housekeeping supplies expense, food expense, liquor expense, wages expense, office supplies expense, repairs and maintenance expense, and heat, light, and power expense. Be certain to label all your expense accounts with the word "expense" so that you do not confuse them with asset accounts. For example, "food account" is a meaningless term. You should label it "food expense" or "food inventory," depending upon which account you are describing.

The money values of debits and credits in all transactions must be equal. Refer again to Figure 1.1. In the first transaction we would debit cash for $5,000 and credit capital to show increases in cash and capital. In the second transaction we would debit food inventory and credit cash for $400 to show an increase in one asset and a decrease in another. In the third transaction we would debit housekeeping supplies inventory and credit accounts payable for $200 to show increases in both an asset and a liability account. In transaction 4 we would debit accounts payable and credit cash to show decreases in a liability and an asset account. Transaction 5 would involve two sets of entries. First we would debit cash and credit food sales for $400 to show increases in an asset account and an income account. Second, we would debit food expense and credit food inventory for $100 to show an increase in an expense account and a decrease in an asset account.

THE ACCOUNTING CYCLE

The work of an accountant is organized so that he goes through the same routine each time the books are totaled and financial statements are drawn up. The routine is called the *accounting cycle*. It begins with the first journal entry at the beginning of the financial period and ends with the post-closing trial balance at the end of the financial period. We will continue our review of basic accounting by going through the complete accounting cycle using only a general journal and general ledger.

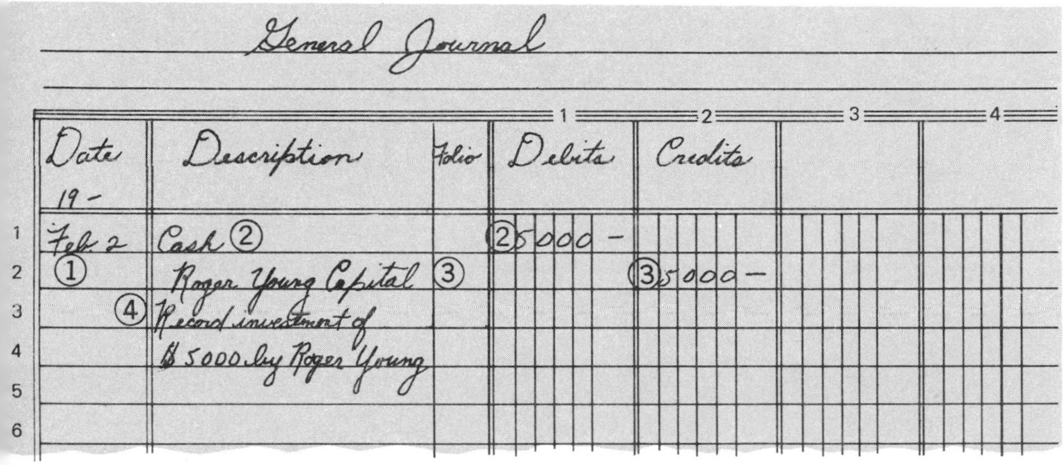

FIGURE 1.2. THE PROCEDURE FOR JOURNALIZING TRANSACTIONS.

Journalizing

The first step in the accounting cycle is to enter transactions into the journal. This procedure is called *journalizing*. The form of the general journal should already be familiar to you. It is illustrated in Figure 1.2 along with the following steps in journalizing:

1. Enter the date of the transaction. The month needs to be entered

on each page only once. It is assumed that the next transaction will have occurred in the same month unless a new month is entered.

2. Record the debit entry. Start writing at the left-hand margin of the description column. Enter the amount in the debit column.
3. Record the credit entry. Indent about a quarter of an inch. Enter the amount in the credit column.
4. Write the explanation for the entry on the next line below the credit entry.

Sometimes a transaction will involve more than one account to be debited or credited. The procedure for journalizing will not change; we simply must remember to enter all debits before we enter credit entries. Figure 1.3 illustrates the procedure for journalizing a more complex entry.

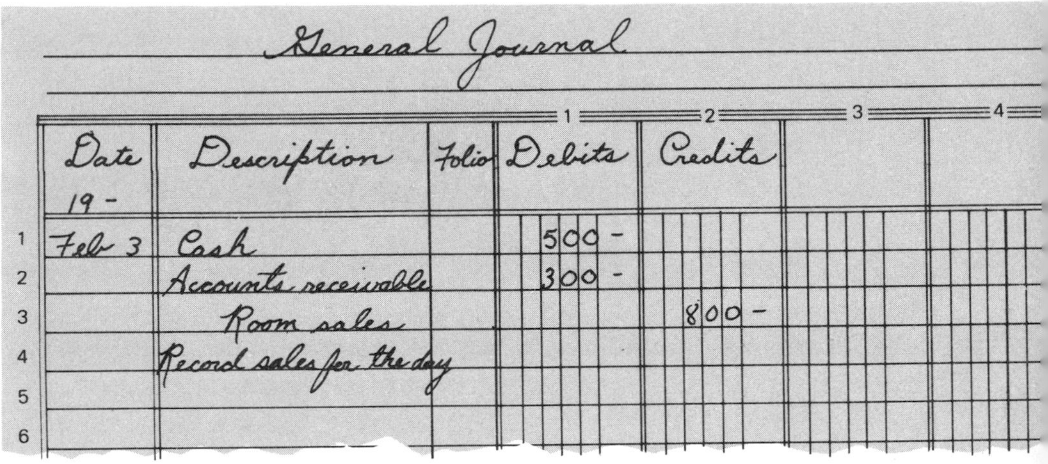

General Journal

Date	Description	Folio	Debits	Credits		
19 -						
Feb 3	Cash		500 -			
	Accounts receivable		300 -			
	Room sales			800 -		
	Record sales for the day					

FIGURE 1.3. THE PROCEDURE FOR JOURNALIZING COMPLEX ENTRIES.

The following transactions occurred when Roger Young purchased a hotel. Figure 1.4 illustrates the journal entries for the transactions. Study all entries carefully and be sure to ask your instructor about any of them that you do not understand.

June 1. Mr. Young invests $100,000 into the business.

June 2. A hotel is purchased with the funds. The building is valued at $50,000, land at $25,000, and furniture and fixtures at $25,000.

June 3. Mr. Young signs a 90-day note at the First National Bank. He receives $10,000 which he will use for working capital. Interest on the note will be 6 percent.

June 4. The hotel purchases $500 worth of food on account from Glick Purveyors.

June 4. The hotel purchases $350 worth of liquor for cash.

June 5. The hotel purchases $200 worth of housekeeping supplies on account from Janitorial Supplies, Inc.

June 5. The hotel purchases $300 worth of office supplies for cash.

June 6. Sales for the day as follows: room sales, $550; food sales, $320; liquor sales, $150. $420 was received in cash. The balance was charged to guest accounts.

June 6. Expenses incurred for the day as follows: food used from inventory, $80; liquor used from inventory, $30.

June 7. Sales for the day as follows: room sales, $530; food sales, $340; liquor sales, $160. $490 was received in cash. The balance was charged to guest accounts.

June 7. Expenses incurred for the day as follows: food used from inventory, $100; liquor used from inventory, $35.

June 7. The hotel receives $600 in cash from guests who previously charged rooms, food, and liquor.

June 7. The hotel pays Glick Purveyors' food bill incurred June 4.

June 7. The hotel pays cash wages of $250.

Posting to Ledger Accounts

The next step in the accounting cycle is to post all journal entries to ledger accounts. The steps in posting are as follows:

1. Enter the date as it appears in the journal entry.
2. Enter the amount in the appropriate debit or credit column.
3. Enter the page number of the journal entry in the column labeled "folio."
4. Go back to the journal and enter the account number in the column labeled "folio."

No entry need be made in the "item" column if the entry is covered by an appropriate explanation in the journal.

Figure 1.5 shows how a transaction is posted from the journal to a ledger account.

Roger Young's Hotel
General Journal   Page 1

Date 19—	Description	Folio	Debits	Credits		
June 1	Cash		100000 —			
	Roger Young Capital			100000 —		
	Record investment of					
	$100,000 by Roger Young					
2	Building		50000 —			
	Land		25000 —			
	Furniture and fixtures		25000 —			
	Cash			100000 —		
	Purchase of hotel and					
	property					
3	Cash		10000 —			
	Notes payable			10000 —		
	Borrowed $10000 from					
	First National Bank on					
	90-day note @ 6% interest					
4	Food inventory		500 —			
	Accounts payable			500 —		
	Purchased food from					
	Glick purveyors					
4	Liquor inventory		350 —			
	Cash			350 —		
	Purchase liquor for cash					
5	Housekeeping supplies					
	inventory		200 —			
	Accounts payable			200 —		
	Purchase supplies from					
	Junatorial Supplies Inc.					

FIGURE 1.4.   JOURNAL ENTRIES FOR THE TRANSACTIONS OF ROGER YOUNG'S HOTEL.

General Journal   Page 2

Date 19—	Description	Folio	Debits	Credits		
June 5	Office supplies					
	inventory		300 —			
	Cash			300 —		
	Purchase office					
	supplies for cash					
6	Cash		420 —			
	Accounts receivable		600 —			
	Food sales			320 —		
	Room sales			550 —		
	Liquor sales			150 —		
	Room, food and liquor					
	sales for the day					
6	Food expense		80 —			
	Liquor expense		30 —			
	Food inventory			80 —		
	Liquor inventory			30 —		
	Food and liquor used					
	from inventories					
7	Cash		490 —			
	Accounts receivable		540 —			
	Room sales			530 —		
	Food sales			340 —		
	Liquor sales			160 —		
	Room, food and liquor					
	sales for the day					
7	Food expense		100 —			
	Liquor expense		35 —			
	Food inventory			100 —		

			1	2	3	4
	General Journal			Page 3		
Date	Description	Folio	Debits	Credits		
June 7	Liquor inventory			35 –		
	Food and liquor used					
	from inventories					
7	Cash		600 =			
	Accounts receivable			600 –		
	Cash received from					
	guests on account					
7	Accounts payable		500 –			
	Cash			500 –		
	Pay black purveyors					
	for food purchased 6/4					
7	Wages expense		250 –			
	Cash			250 –		
	Wages paid for					
	period 6/4 to 6/7					

FIGURE 1.4. (Continued.)

Account Numbers

Every business will have its own set of account numbers. Similar accounts will have similar numbers so that one can tell the kind of account by looking at the number. This text will use the following sets of numbers:

Table 1.2. ACCOUNT NUMBERS

Account Name	Account Number
Current assets	100—149
Fixed assets	150—199
Current liabilities	200—249
Long-term liabilities	250—299
Capital	300—399
Income accounts	400—499
Expense accounts	500—599
Other accounts	600—699

FIGURE 1.5. PROCEDURE FOR POSTING TRANSACTIONS FROM THE JOURNAL TO LEDGER ACCOUNTS.

ACCOUNT NO. 100

TERMS — NAME Cash
RATING — ADDRESS
CREDIT LIMIT

DATE 19	ITEMS	FOLIO	✓	DEBITS	DATE 19	ITEMS	FOLIO	✓	CREDITS
June 1		g1		100000 —	June 2		g1		100000
3		g1		10000 —	4		g1		350
6		g2		420 —	5		g2		300
7		g2		490 —	7		g3		500
7	10,110 —	g3		600 —	7		g3		250
				111510					101400

ACCOUNT NO. 103

TERMS — NAME Accounts Receivable
RATING — ADDRESS
CREDIT LIMIT

DATE 19	ITEMS	FOLIO	✓	DEBITS	DATE 19	ITEMS	FOLIO	✓	CREDITS
June 6		g2		600 —	June 7		g3		600 —
7	540 —	g2		540 —					
				1140					

ACCOUNT NO. 111

TERMS — NAME Office Supplies Inventory
RATING — ADDRESS
CREDIT LIMIT

DATE 19	ITEMS	FOLIO	✓	DEBITS	DATE 19	ITEMS	FOLIO	✓	CREDITS
June 5		g2		300 —					

ACCOUNT NO. 120

TERMS — NAME Food Inventory
RATING — ADDRESS
CREDIT LIMIT

DATE 19	ITEMS	FOLIO	✓	DEBITS	DATE 19	ITEMS	FOLIO	✓	CREDITS
June 4	320	g1		500 —	June 6		g2		80 —
					7		g2		100 —
									180

ACCOUNT NO. 130

TERMS — NAME Liquor Inventory
RATING — ADDRESS
CREDIT LIMIT

DATE 19	ITEMS	FOLIO	✓	DEBITS	DATE 19	ITEMS	FOLIO	✓	CREDITS
June 4	285	g1		350 —	June 6		g2		30 —
							g3		35 —
									65

FIGURE 1.6.   THE LEDGER ACCOUNTS FOR ROGER YOUNG'S HOTEL.

SHEET NO.					ACCOUNT NO. 140					
TERMS			NAME	Housekeeping Supplies Inventory						
RATING			ADDRESS							
CREDIT LIMIT										
DATE 19	ITEMS	FOLIO /	DEBITS	DATE 19	ITEMS		FOLIO /	CREDITS		
June 5		J1	200 —							

SHEET NO.					ACCOUNT NO. 151					
TERMS			NAME	Building						
RATING			ADDRESS							
CREDIT LIMIT										
DATE 19	ITEMS	FOLIO /	DEBITS	DATE 19	ITEMS		FOLIO /	CREDITS		
June 2		J1	50000 —							

SHEET NO.					ACCOUNT NO. 161					
TERMS			NAME	Land						
RATING			ADDRESS							
CREDIT LIMIT										
DATE 19	ITEMS	FOLIO /	DEBITS	DATE 19	ITEMS		FOLIO /	CREDITS		
June 2		J1	25000 —							

SHEET NO.					ACCOUNT NO. 171					
TERMS			NAME	Furniture and Fixtures						
RATING			ADDRESS							
CREDIT LIMIT										
DATE 19	ITEMS	FOLIO /	DEBITS	DATE 19	ITEMS		FOLIO /	CREDITS		
June 2		J1	25000 —							

SHEET NO.					ACCOUNT NO. 202					
TERMS			NAME	Notes Payable						
RATING			ADDRESS							
CREDIT LIMIT										
DATE 19	ITEMS	FOLIO /	DEBITS	DATE 19	ITEMS		FOLIO /	CREDITS		
				June 3			J1	10000 —		

SHEET NO. _____   ACCOUNT NO. _204_

TERMS _____   NAME   Accounts Payable

RATING _____   ADDRESS

CREDIT LIMIT _____

DATE 19	ITEMS	FOLIO	/	DEBITS	DATE 19	ITEMS	FOLIO	/	CREDITS
June 7		J3		500 —	June 4		J1		500
					5	200	J1		200
									700

SHEET NO. _____   ACCOUNT NO. _300_

TERMS _____   NAME   Roger Young Capital

RATING _____   ADDRESS

CREDIT LIMIT _____

DATE 19	ITEMS	FOLIO	/	DEBITS	DATE 19	ITEMS	FOLIO	/	CREDITS
					June 1		J1		100000 —

SHEET NO. _____   ACCOUNT NO. _401_

TERMS _____   NAME   Room Sales

RATING _____   ADDRESS

CREDIT LIMIT _____

DATE 19	ITEMS	FOLIO	/	DEBITS	DATE 19	ITEMS	FOLIO	/	CREDITS
					June 6		J2		550 —
					7		J2		530 —
									1080

SHEET NO. _____   ACCOUNT NO. _421_

TERMS _____   NAME   Food Sales

RATING _____   ADDRESS

CREDIT LIMIT _____

DATE 19	ITEMS	FOLIO	/	DEBITS	DATE 19	ITEMS	FOLIO	/	CREDITS
					June 6		J2		320 —
					7		J2		340 —
									660

FIGURE 1.6. (Continued.)

SHEET NO. _____   ACCOUNT NO. 481

TERMS   NAME   Liquor Sales
RATING   ADDRESS
CREDIT LIMIT

DATE 19	ITEMS	FOLIO	/	DEBITS	DATE 19	ITEMS	FOLIO	/	CREDITS
					June 6		J 2		150 —
					7		J 2		160 —
									310

SHEET NO. _____   ACCOUNT NO. 522

TERMS   NAME   Food Expense
RATING   ADDRESS
CREDIT LIMIT

DATE 19	ITEMS	FOLIO	/	DEBITS	DATE 19	ITEMS	FOLIO	/	CREDITS
June 6		J 2		80 —					
7		J 2		100 —					
				180					

SHEET NO. _____   ACCOUNT NO. 532

TERMS   NAME   Liquor Expense
RATING   ADDRESS
CREDIT LIMIT

DATE 19	ITEMS	FOLIO	/	DEBITS	DATE 19	ITEMS	FOLIO	/	CREDITS
June 6		J 2		30 —					
7		J 2		35 —					
				65					

SHEET NO. _____   ACCOUNT NO. 545

TERMS   NAME   Wages Expense
RATING   ADDRESS
CREDIT LIMIT

DATE 19	ITEMS	FOLIO	/	DEBITS	DATE 19	ITEMS	FOLIO	/	CREDITS
June 7		J 3		250 —					

You will observe that we have set aside many more numbers than we will use. However, this is all right because now we will be able to recognize an asset, liability, capital, income, or expense account merely by looking at its number.

Figure 1.6 shows the transactions from Roger Young's journal posted to ledger accounts.

Trial Balance

When all transactions from the journal have been posted, the accounts are added and the balances are transferred to the work sheet. We were very careful to post equal amounts to the debit and credit columns of our journal. Consequently the sum of all accounts with debit balances in the ledger should equal the sum of all accounts with credit balances. We have a trial balance when we have proven debits equal credits by adding all the account balances on our work sheet.

The accounts are listed on our work sheet in a specific order. Asset accounts are listed first. They are followed by liabilities, capital, income, and expense accounts. The reason for listing them in that fashion will be explained when we discuss the income and balance sheet columns of the work sheet.

Most students make at least one arithmetical mistake while attempting to obtain a trial balance. If the total debits do not agree with the total credits, use the following procedure to find your mistake:

1. Readd the debit and credit columns of your trial balance.
2. Verify that all ledger accounts have been entered on your work sheet and that the balances as shown have been properly transferred to the work sheet.
3. Readd all ledger accounts.
4. Recheck your postings to be sure you posted correctly all entries from the journal.
5. Verify that you journalized equal debits and credits.

Columns 1 and 2 in Figure 1.7 show the trial balance for Roger Young's Hotel. The ledger accounts show the proper way to obtain account balances.

Adjustments and Adjusted Trial Balance

Adjusting entries are planned corrections to ledger accounts, and they are made after the trial balance on our work sheet. We will journalize them and post the journal entries to ledger accounts later. You will recall from your work in basic accounting that there are many kinds of adjusting entries. We may adjust our inventory account balances to bring them into line with the actual values of our inventories. We may record the decrease in value of some of our fixed assets over the past financial period. We may record any expenses that occurred which we have not recognized during the financial period. Or we may find it necessary to correct one or more accounts due to errors during the month. The purpose of the adjusting entries is to have financial records that are as accurate as we can possibly get them.

The following adjustments were made to the accounts of Roger Young's Hotel.

1. A physical inventory of food shows its actual value is $310.
2. A physical inventory of liquor shows its actual value is $280.
3. A physical inventory of housekeeping supplies shows its actual value is $150.
4. A physical inventory of office supplies shows its actual value is $275.
5. The building has depreciated $50 during the past financial period.

Columns 3 and 4 in Figure 1.7 show the above adjusting entries.

We then combine the adjustments columns on the work sheet with the original trial balance columns to arrive at an adjusted trial balance. We must add entries if they are both in debit columns, and we must subtract entries if they are in differently labeled columns. Totals are again taken to assure us that we have done our work correctly. The adjusted trial balance for Roger Young's Hotel is shown in columns 5 and 6.

Income Statement and Balance Sheet

We took great pains to list our accounts on the work sheet in numerical order. Now our efforts will pay off. The next step in the accounting cycle is to transfer those account balances that belong in our income statement to the "income statement" portion of the work sheet and to transfer those account balances that belong in our balance sheet to the "balance sheet" portion of the work sheet. This process is very easy because we simply transfer those account balances with 100, 200, and 300 series account numbers to the balance sheet portion of the work sheet, and we transfer those account balances with 400 and 500 account numbers to the income portion of our work sheet. Because we listed our accounts on the work sheet in numerical order, those accounts on the top half of our work sheet will go to the balance sheet portion of the work sheet. All the accounts on the bottom half of the work sheet, with the exception of an adjusting entry or two, will go to the income statement portion of the work sheet.

Work Sheet — Roger

	Account No.	Name	Trial Balance Debit	Trial Balance Credit	Adjustments Debit	Adjustments Credit
1	100	Cash	10110 -			
2	103	Accounts receivable	540 -			
3	111	Office Supplies Inventory	300 -			(4) 25 -
4	120	Food Inventory	320 -			(1) 10 -
5	130	Liquor Inventory	285 -			(2) 5 -
6	140	Housekeeping Supplies Inventory	200 -			(3) 50 -
7	151	Building	50000 -			
8	161	Land	25000 -			
9	171	Furniture and Fixtures	25000 -			
10	202	Notes Payable		10000 -		
11	204	Accounts Payable		200 -		
12	300	Roger Young capital		100000 -		
13	401	Room Sales		1080 -		
14	421	Food Sales		660 -		
15	431	Liquor Sales		310 -		
16	522	Food Expense	180 -		(1) 10 -	
17	532	Liquor Expense	65 -		(2) 5 -	
18	545	Wages Expense	250 -			
19			112250 -	112250 -		
20						
21	550	Housekeeping Supplies Expense			(3) 50 -	
22	560	Office Supplies Expense			(4) 25 -	
23	540	Depreciation Expense			(5) 50 -	
24	152	Accumulated Depreciation-Bldg.				50
25					140	140
26		Net Profit				
27						
28						
29						

FIGURE 1.7. THE WORK SHEET FOR ROGER YOUNG'S HOTEL.

Young's Hotel

	5	6	7	8	9	10	11	12	
	Adjusted Trial Balance		Income Statement		Balance Sheet				
	Debit	Credit	Debit	Credit	Debit	Credit			
1	10110 -				10110 -				
2	540 -				540 -				
3	275 -				275 -				
4	310 -				310 -				
5	280 -				280 -				
6	150 -				150 -				
7	50000 -				50000 -				
8	25000 -				25000 -				
9	25000 -				25000 -				
10		10000				10000			
11		200				200			
12		100000				100000 -			
13		1080 -		1080 -					
14		660 -		660 -					
15		310 -		310 -					
16	190 -		190 -						
17	70 -		70 -						
18	250 -		250 -						
19									
20									
21	50 -		50 -						
22	25 -		25 -						
23	50 -		50 -						
24		50 -				50 -			
25	112300	112300	635	2050					
26			1415			1415 -			
27			2050	2050	111665 -	111665 -			
28									
29									
30									

To determine our profit for the period we add up the debit and credit columns on the income statement portion of the work sheet. The difference between the two columns is our profit and will be the amount we will transfer to our balance sheet. The net profit will be just enough to balance our new balance sheet.

The income statement and balance sheet portions of Roger Young's Hotel are shown in the last four columns of Figure 1.7.

We now have all the information needed to prepare a formal income statement and a formal balance sheet. Both of these statements are prepared now rather than after we close the books because manage-

Statement of Income

Roger Young's Hotel

Month of June 19 —

Operated departments	Net Sales	Cost of Sales	Payroll and related expenses	Other expenses	Profit
Rooms	$1,080		$100	$50	$930
Food	660	$190	100		370
Beverage	310	70	50		190
	$2,050	$260	$250	$50	$1,490
Gross operating income					$1,490
Deductions from income					
Office supplies expense					25
Gross operating profit					$1,465
Less depreciation expense					50
Net profit to capital					$1,415

FIGURE 1.8.   INCOME STATEMENT FOR ROGER YOUNG'S HOTEL.

Balance Sheet

Roger Young's Hotel

As of June 30, 19 __

ASSETS

Current assets

Cash	$10,110	
Accounts Receivable	540	
Office supplies	275	
Food inventory	310	
Housekeeping supplies	150	
Liquor inventory	280	

Total current assets $ 11,665

Fixed assets

Land		$25,000
Building	$50,000	
Less depreciation	50	49,950
Furniture & Fixtures		25,000

Total fixed assets $ 99,950

Total assets $111,615

LIABILITIES AND CAPITAL

Current liabilities

Notes payable	$10,000
Accounts payable	200

Total current liabilities $ 10,200

Capital

Roger Young Capital	
June 1, 19 __	$100,000
Add profit	1,415

Total capital $101,415

Total liabilities and capital $111,615

FIGURE 1.9.   BALANCE SHEET FOR ROGER YOUNG'S HOTEL.

General Journal   Page 3

Date	Description	Folio	Debit	Credit		
19 –						
	Adjusting Entries					
June 30	Food expense	522	10 –			
	Food inventory	120		10 –		
	Liquor expense	532	5 –			
	Liquor inventory	130		5 –		
	Housekeeping supplies expense	550	50 –			
	Housekeeping supplies inventory	140		50 –		
	Office supplies expense	560	25 –			
	Office supplies inventory	111		25 –		
	Depreciation expense	540	50 –			
	Accumulated depreciation – Bldg.	152		50 –		
	Closing Entries					
June 30	Income and expense summary	610	635 –			
	Food expense	522		190 –		
	Liquor expense	532		70 –		
	Wages expense	545		250 –		
	Housekeeping supplies expense	550		50 –		

FIGURE 1.10.   ADJUSTING AND CLOSING ENTRIES FOR ROGER YOUNG'S HOTEL.

General Journal   Page 4

Date 19–	Description	Folio	Debit	Credit	3	4
June 30	Office supplies expense	560		25 –		
	Depreciation expense	540		50 –		
	Room sales	401	1080 –			
	Food sales	421	660 –			
	Liquor sales	431	310 –			
	Income and expense summary	610		2050 –		
	Income and expense summary	610	1415 –			
	Roger Young, capital	300		1415 –		

FIGURE 1.10. (Continued.)

ment is anxious to get the information contained in them. The formal income statement and balance sheet are illustrated in Figures 1.8 and 1.9. The form of the income statement will perhaps look considerably different from any other you have seen. Do not be concerned if you do not completely understand it at this point. We will go into it in detail in a later chapter.

Journalizing and Posting Adjusting and Closing Entries

The remaining steps in the accounting cycle are designed to get our ledger accounts ready for the new accounting period. We will journalize entries already made on the work sheet, formally transfer the profit to Roger Young's capital account, and we will rule our ac-

FIGURE 1.11. CLOSING ENTRIES POSTED TO SELECTED ACCOUNTS.

SHEET NO. _____									ACCOUNT NO. _522_	
TERMS			NAME	*Food Expense*						
RATING			ADDRESS							
CREDIT LIMIT										
DATE 19		ITEMS	FOLIO	✓	DEBITS	DATE 19	ITEMS	FOLIO	✓	CREDITS
June	6		J2		80 —	June 30	closing	J3		190 —
	7		J2		100 —					
					180 —					
	30	adjusting	J3		10 —					
					190 —					190 —

SHEET NO. _____									ACCOUNT NO. _610_	
TERMS			NAME	*Income and Expense Summary*						
RATING			ADDRESS							
CREDIT LIMIT										
DATE 19		ITEMS	FOLIO	✓	DEBITS	DATE 19	ITEMS	FOLIO	✓	CREDITS
June	30	closing	J3		635 —	June 30	closing	J4		2050 —
	30	closing	J4		1415 —					
					2050 —					2050 —

FIGURE 1.11. (Continued.)

counts so that there will be no question where one financial period ends and the next one begins.

The adjusting and closing entries for Roger Young's Hotel are journalized in Figure 1.10, and selected accounts are posted in Figure 1.11. The adjusting journal entries should be obvious to you. However, the closing entries will need explanation.

Closing entries perform two important accounting functions. They zero our income and expense accounts so that we can start them without balances next month, and they enable us to transfer profit to the capital account. It is necessary to open a special account called "income and expense summary account" to perform these two functions. We will use the following procedure:

1. Credit all expense accounts for their balances, and debit income and expense summary account for the total of all expenses.
2. Debit all income accounts for their balances, and credit income and expense summary account for the sum of all income accounts.

3. Zero the income and expense summary account, and transfer net profit to capital by debiting income and expense summary account for the amount of the profit and crediting the capital account for the same amount.

Note that income and expense summary account was a temporary account. We opened it and closed it practically at the same time. All our income and expense accounts now read zero. The only accounts with balances are those listed on the balance sheet.

Post-closing Trial Balance

Account no.	Name	Debit	Credit
100	Cash	10110 —	
103	Accounts receivable	540 —	
111	Office supplies inventory	275 —	
120	Food inventory	310 —	
130	Liquor inventory	280 —	
140	Housekeeping supplies inventory	150 —	
151	Building	50000 —	
152	Accumulated depreciation—Bldg.		50 —
161	Land	25000 —	
171	Furniture and fixtures	25000 —	
202	Notes payable		10000 —
204	Accounts payable		200 —
300	Roger Young capital		101415 —
		111665 —	111665 —

FIGURE 1.12. POST-CLOSING TRIAL BALANCE.

Ruling and Balancing Ledger Accounts

The next-to-the-last step in the accounting cycle is to rule and balance our ledger accounts. Some of our accounts have balances that must be carried forward to the next month, and some have no balances. To rule an account with no balance, we simply draw double lines under the last entries on both sides. Accounts with balances to be carried forward to the next month must be ruled in such a fashion as to show those balances. Figure 1.11 illustrates both of these procedures.

Post-closing Trial Balance

The final step in the accounting cycle is to take a trial balance of all the accounts. We do this to ascertain that we have closed our accounts correctly and that we will start with a proper trial balance at the beginning of the next accounting period. Asset, liability, and capital accounts generally will have balances at this point. No income or expense accounts will have balances. The post-closing trial balance for Roger Young's Hotel is illustrated in Figure 1.12.

SUMMARY

The basic accounting relationship is:

$$\text{Assets} = \text{liabilities} + \text{capital}$$

Assets are defined as something of value owned by a business, liabilities are the creditors' claims upon the assets of the business, and capital is the ownership claim on the assets of the business.

The fundamental equation is altered by the transactions that take place during the normal operations of the business. We ordinarily change the fundamental equation by (1) increasing or decreasing the owner's investment, (2) exchanging one asset for another asset, (3) purchasing an asset on account, (4) paying our debts, and (5) making a profit or loss. The changes that take place in the fundamental equation are reflected in the money values of the various accounts of the business. The accounts are called ledger accounts and are increased or decreased by debit and credit entries. A debit entry is made to the left-hand side of a ledger account and a credit entry is made to the right-hand side of a ledger account. Debits and credits can increase or decrease the values of ledger accounts, depending upon which account we are describing. Asset accounts and expense accounts are increased by debit entries and decreased by credit entries. Liability accounts, capital accounts, and income accounts are increased by credit entries and decreased by debit entries.

The work of an accountant is organized so that he goes through the same routine each financial period. The routine is called the accounting cycle and consists of the following steps.

1. Journalizing or entering transactions into a journal. A journal is a book of original entry.
2. Posting journal entries to ledger accounts.
3. Totaling ledger accounts and preparing a trial balance on the work sheet.
4. Making adjustment entries on the work sheet.
5. Combining the adjusting entries with the original trial balance to obtain an adjusted trial balance.
6. Completing the work sheet by transferring all income and expense account balances to the income portion of the work sheet, and the asset, liability, and capital account balances to the balance sheet portion of the work sheet.
7. Preparing the formal income statement and formal balance sheet.
8. Journalizing and posting the adjusting and closing entries.
9. Ruling and balancing all ledger accounts.
10. Preparing a post-closing trial balance.

QUESTIONS FOR DISCUSSION

1. List and explain the steps in the accounting cycle.
2. Why do we list accounts in numerical order on the work sheet?
3. To correct errors in our ledger accounts we make adjusting entries. Why don't we erase our mistakes instead of making adjusting entries?
4. Explain why the numerical difference between the two columns of the income statement portion of the work sheet is always the exact amount that will balance our new balance sheet.
5. Why do we wait until the formal income statement and balance sheet are prepared before we journalize and post our adjusting entries?
6. Why is it necessary to prepare a post-closing trial balance?
7. The last adjusting entry to Roger Young's accounts was a debit to depreciation expense and a credit to accumulated depreciation— building. Why did we not credit the building account directly?
8. Why would a physical inventory of food or liquor show a different figure than was shown on the books?
9. Explain why most adjusting entries are not made until after the trial balance is prepared.
10. Explain why every transaction affects more than one account.

2 | Accounting for Sales

Our system of keeping track of transactions is satisfactory providing there are not too many transactions. However, one can imagine the problems that would arise using our present system of keeping records if there were several hundred transactions each day. For example, if we were to write out an average of only ten checks each day, our cash ledger account would become hopelessly complicated, and by the end of the month it would be extremely difficult to obtain a balance. Further, our ledger account would have so many entries we would have room on each page for only three or four days' entries.

We need to develop a system that will enable us to post to our ledger accounts in one figure the sum of all transactions for a period of time (for example, one month) and yet retain in our records enough detail to trace the individual transactions. We do this by creating special records called *subsidiary journals*. These journals will serve the same purpose as our general journal. However, we will post the *totals* of our journals to the ledger accounts once each month instead of posting the individual transactions, as was the case with our general journal. The subsidiary journals will be set up in such a fashion that frequently occurring transactions of a similar nature will be journalized in only one journal. We will have a subsidiary journal for income, one for cash received, one for cash paid out, one for purchases, and so on. We will no longer use our general journal to record transactions that fit into our subsidiary journals.

We will begin by discussing the special journals used to record income.

FIGURE 2.1. THE TOTALED GUEST CHECK.

Guest Check

No. of Cks.	Table	No. Persons	Server	Book & Check No.
	4	2	A	4688 8
1	T juice			
1	consomme			
1	Steak rare			6 50
1	Roast beef			5 50
2	Corn			
2	Baked pot.			
2	Coffee			
				$ 12 00
			TAX	60
				$ 12 60

PLEASE PAY CASHIER

17RC ① No. 32

Guest Check

No. of Cks.	Table	No. Persons	Server	Book & Check No.
	6	3	A	4688 10
2	Consomme			
1	Grapefruit juice			
1	Roast lamb			4 50
2	Steak rare			13 —
1	Corn			
2	Peas			
3	Baked pot.			
3	Drinks			4 —
				2 50
	B. Glickman		TAX	1 08
	#214			22 58

PLEASE PAY CASHIER

17RC ① No. 32

ACCOUNTING FOR RESTAURANT AND BAR SALES

Sales in the restaurant are first recorded when the waiter takes the order for food or liquor. He writes the order on a guest check. The guest check is priced and totaled by a food checker, waiter, or cashier. The customer eats his meal and is presented with his totaled bill by the waiter (Figure 2.1).

He pays his bill or charges it to his account at the restaurant cashier's station. The restaurant cashier enters the information on the *restaurant cashier's sheet* (Figure 2.2). The restaurant cashier's sheet is really a journal because it is a book of original entry. However, it is one of our special columnar journals because it records only sales of food and liquor. Note that it does not have the appearance of the journals we are accustomed to seeing. The charge sales are immediately sent to the front office to be recorded on guest bills. We do it at once because there is a possibility guests may check out of the hotel soon after eating. If the charge does not arrive at the front desk before the guest leaves the hotel, we may not be able to collect.

The cashier totals and balances the restaurant cashier's sheet after all customers have left the restaurant. The formula for balancing it is

Cash + charges = food sales + beverage sales + sales tax

He verifies that all guest checks are accounted for by checking the numbers of the checks received with the list of numbers of the checks issued to the waiters. The checks, cashier's sheet, and money taken in are brought to the front office and turned over to the front office cashier. The front office cashier puts the money in her cash drawer and records the amount received on the *front office cash sheet* (Figure 2.3).

The totals of the restaurant cashier's sheet will later be posted to the summary sales journal. We are already beginning to achieve the results desired from subsidiary journals. All the sales in the restaurant have been nicely summarized so that we do not have to work with individual sales but can work with total restaurant sales, total accounts receivable, and total cash. Yet the detailed information will always be recorded on the restaurant cashier's sheet should we want to refer to it.

Many restaurants do not use a restaurant cashier's sheet as illustrated, but instead use a cash register of some type. Accounting for restaurant sales using a machine is no different from the manual method. The machine does all the pricing and adding for us, and the totals come from the machine simply by pressing the total buttons. There are obvious advantages to using the machine. Of importance to the accountant is the machine's greater accuracy and better control.

No Persons	Name	Check no.	Waiter no.	Cash	Charge
2		4688 1	A	12 60	
3	B. Glickman	4688 2	A		22 58
2	J. Sunshine	4687 1	B		15 75
4		4687 2	B	36 75	
1		4689 1	C	5 83	
4		4688 3	A	25 20	
4	P. Gould	4689 2	C		39 39
6		4687 3	B	41 48	
1	G. Barry	4688 4	A		7 35
3		4689 3	C	17 85	
30				139 71	85 07
			cash	139 71	
			charge	85 07	
				224 78	

FIGURE 2.2. THE RESTAURANT CASHIER'S SHEET.

Bar sales are recorded in the same way as restaurant sales. All orders are written on guest checks and entered on the bar cashier's sheet or rung through a cash register. The bar cashier's sheet or cash register is totaled (Figure 2.4). The cash, charges, and cashier's sheet are sent to the front office where the cashier records the amount received on her front office cash sheet and where charges are posted to guest accounts.

ACCOUNTING FOR ROOM SALES

Guests checking into the hotel fill out registration cards showing name, address, and other information the hotel wants for its records. The room clerk will use the information on the registration cards to prepare guest bills, room rack cards, information rack cards, and check-in notices for various departments in the hotel. The room rack card is particularly important to the accounting department, because

Hotel
Cashier's Sheet — June 1, 19—

Food sales	Beverage sales	Sales tax	Sundry					
12 —		60						1
17 50	4 —	1 08						2
13 —	2 —	75						3
26 50	8 50	1 75						4
4 30	1 25	28						5
24 —		1 20						6
28 50	9 —	1 89						7
32 —	7 50	1 98						8
6 —	1 —	35						9
17 —		85						10
180 80	33 25	$10 73						11
								12
180 80	Food sales							13
33 25	Beverage sales							14
10 73	Sales tax							15
224 78								16

the *room clerk's daily revenue report* will be prepared from the information on it. A registration card, rack card, and room clerk's daily revenue report are illustrated in Figures 2.5 and 2.6.

Each evening the room clerk on duty will prepare the room clerk's daily revenue report from the information on the rack cards. The revenue report is verified by the night auditor with the revenue he has posted to guest folios, and it is sent to the accounting department along with other information from the front office to be posted to the summary sales journal. All room sales are treated as charges to guest accounts, even though guests may pay for rooms at the time of check-in.

ACCOUNTING FOR TELEPHONE SALES

All long-distance calls going through the hotel's switchboard are entered on the *telephone traffic sheet*. The operator prepares charge vouchers (Figure 2.7) for the calls to be charged to guest accounts and sends them to the front office. The telephone traffic sheet is totaled (Figure 2.8), verified by the night auditor, and the totals are posted to the summary sales journals.

Most hotels have newer telephone equipment that automatically monitors outgoing calls and prints out records of charges. The printed record of charge can be used in place of the hand-written voucher.

The front office cashier will post telephone charges to guest bills. Many guests make long-distance calls and immediately thereafter check out of the hotel. It is thus very important that telephone charges be promptly sent to the front office and that the cashier immediately post the charges to guest bills.

ACCOUNTING FOR OTHER SALES DEPARTMENTS IN THE HOTEL

Large hotels have other sales departments, such as a newsstand, barber and beauty shops, valet service, and a drugstore. Each of these departments has its own sales records. In order to keep our work from becoming too complicated, we will not take them into consideration at this time. We should recognize, however, that the sales from these departments would be handled in the same fashion as those from other departments. A charge slip will be made out, the information will be recorded on a journal, and the totals will be posted to the summary sales journal.

THE SUMMARY SALES JOURNAL

All the sales records are gathered together in the accountant's office, audited by the day auditor, and recorded in the *summary sales journal*. Figure 2.9 illustrates the summary sales journal for Roger Young's Hotel. The journal will have at least 31 lines, one for each day of the month. Each day the sales information for that day is put on one line in the sales journal. At the end of the month, the sales journal is totaled and balanced and the total figures are posted to general ledger accounts. The journal is balanced the same way we balanced the restaurant cashier's sheet. Total sales from the various departments must equal total cash received plus the total charged to guest accounts.

The summary sales journal is posted as follows. The room sales column, total food sales column, total bar sales column, and telephone sales column are posted as credits to their sales accounts in the ledger. The sales tax column is posted as a credit to sales taxes payable, a

WM. ALLEN & CO., N. Y. STOCK FORM 8122

Front Office Cashier's Receipts and Disbursements

CASHIER Margaret Rogers   WATCH _____

DATE June 1 _____ 12 _____

No. 1

ROOM NO.	ACC'T NO.	NAME	RECEIPTS		ROOM NO.	ACC'T NO.	NAME		DISBURSEMENTS		
			GUESTS	OTHER				DETAIL	GUESTS	HOUSE	
		Cash Sales DR									
		Food 115.80									
		Liquor 17.25									
		Tax 6.66		139 71							
		Cash Sales Bar									
		Food 0.00									
		Liquor 28.65									
		Tax 1.50		31 15							
				170 86							

RECAPITULATION

TOTAL RECEIPTS

DISBURSEMENTS—GUESTS

DISBURSEMENTS—HOUSE

TOTAL DISBURSEMENTS

DEPOSIT

FIGURE 2.3.   CASH SALES POSTED TO THE FRONT OFFICE CASH SHEET.

liability account. The total of the accounts receivable column is posted as a debit to the accounts receivable ledger account, and the total of the cash sales column is posted as a debit to an account called exchange. We would not post cash sales to our cash ledger account because all cash sales were also posted to the front office cash sheet and will be recorded in the cash ledger account through the cash receipts journal discussed in the next chapter. However, we do want to post equal debits and credits to our ledger accounts, so we post cash sales to exchange. We will fully discuss this account in the next chapter.

Roger Young's
Bar Cashier's

	No. Persons	Name	Check no.	Waiter no.	Cash	Charge
1	1		5577 1	1	1 05	
2	2		5578 1	2	2 63	
3	2	P Gould	5578 2	2		2 10
4	4		5577 2	1	6 56	
5	2	J. Macey	5578 3	2		4 7.
6	1		5577 3	1	95	
7	3		5577 4	1	4 73	
8	2		5577 5	1	3 15	
9	2	J. Grace	5578 4	2		6 3
10	6		5577 6	1	12 08	
11					31 15	1 3
12						
13					31 15	
14					1 3 13	
15					44 28	
16						
17						
18						
19						

FIGURE 2.4.   THE BAR CASHIER'S SHEET.

We have overcome the problem of keeping clutter out of the ledger accounts, yet we have retained sufficient detail to trace all transactions to their source. The department sales records summarize all sales on a daily basis, the summary sales journal summarizes all sales on a monthly basis, and we only have to make one posting to each ledger account from the journal.

One further point should be made about all special journals. You will recall that each transaction in our general journal required an explanation. Our special journals are set up in such a fashion that it is

	Food sales	Beverage sales	Sales tax	Sundry	5	6	7	8	9	10	11	12		
1		1 —	05										
2		2 50	13										
3		2 —	10										
4		6 25	31										
5	3 00	1 50	23										
6		90	05										
7		4 50	23										
8		3 —	15										
9	4 00	2 00	30										
10		11 50	58										
11	7 00	35 15	2 13										
12													
13	7 00												
14	35 15												
15	2 13												
16	44 28												

Hotel Sheet

obvious to any accountant why the postings were made. Therefore, no explanation is needed. If anyone auditing the journals needs information about a transaction, the records are sufficiently clear for him to trace it back to its source.

| 103 | Macey, M/M (2) | $25.00 |
| 6/1 | Boston, Mass 6/3 | |

FIGURE 2.5. THE ROOM RACK CARD (TOP) AND THE COMPLETED REGISTRATION CARD (BOTTOM).

Nọ 0887

Date *June 1, 19—*

NAME *Mr. & Mrs. Joseph Macey*

STREET *1155 Park Street*

CITY *Boston, Mass.*

Money, Jewels and other Valuable Packages, must be placed in the Safe in the Office, otherwise the management will not be responsible for any loss.

ARRIVED	ROOM	RATE	CLERK	DEPARTURE
6/1	*103*	*25 —*	*PRD*	

REMARKS:

WILLIAM ALLEN & CO., N.Y., STOCK FORM 7014½

ROGER YOUNG'S HOTEL

ROOM CLERK'S DAILY REVENUE REPORT

Room No.	No. Persons	Room Rate	Tax	Room No.	No. Persons	Room Rate	Tax
100	3	30—	1.50	200			
101				201	2	25—	1.25
102				202			
103	2	25—	1.25	203	2	25—	1.25
104	2	25—	1.25	204	2	25—	1.25
105	2	25—	1.25	205	3	30—	1.50
106				206	1	20—	1.—
107				207			
108	2	25—	1.25	208	2	25—	1.25
109				209			
110	1	20—	1.00	210	2	25—	1.25
111	2	22—	1.10	211	2	22—	1.10
112				212	3	30—	1.50
114	2	22—	1.10	214			
115	3	30—	1.50	215	2	22—	1.10
116	2	22—	1.10	216	1	20—	1.00
117				217	2	22—	1.10
118	2	22—	1.10	218	2	22—	1.10
119	2	22—	1.10	219	3	30—	1.50
Total	25	$290—	$14.50	Total	29	$343—	$17.15

Total First Floor	25	290—	14.50
Grand Total	54	$633—	$31.65

FIGURE 2.6.   ROOM CLERK'S DAILY REVENUE REPORT.

SUMMARY

The system of keeping track of transactions which we used in Chapter 1 did not provide us with a means of handling large numbers of transactions without our work becoming complicated and cumbersome. So we developed subsidiary journals that enabled us to summarize the transactions each day on one line of a sheet of paper and post monthly totals to our ledger accounts.

The first of the subsidiary journals we discussed was used to record income. Income generated in the dining room and bar is first recorded on guest checks, which are priced and totaled. The guest checks are recorded on the restaurant cashier's sheet and bar cashier's sheet. The totaled information from the various cashiers' sheets is then recorded in the summary sales journal each day. At the end of the month, the journal is totaled and the summary figures for the month are posted to the ledger accounts.

Income generated by room sales is first recorded on guest bills and on

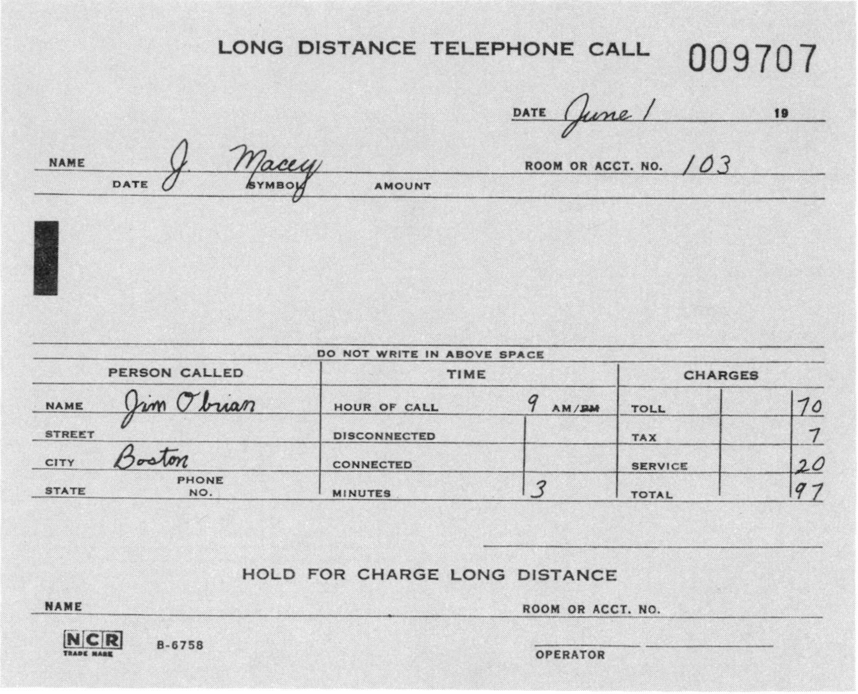

LONG DISTANCE TELEPHONE CALL 009707

DATE June 1 19

NAME J. Macey ROOM OR ACCT. NO. 103

DATE SYMBOL AMOUNT

DO NOT WRITE IN ABOVE SPACE

PERSON CALLED		TIME			CHARGES	
NAME	Jim O'brian	HOUR OF CALL	9 AM/PM	TOLL		70
STREET		DISCONNECTED		TAX		7
CITY	Boston	CONNECTED		SERVICE		20
STATE	PHONE NO.	MINUTES	3	TOTAL		97

HOLD FOR CHARGE LONG DISTANCE

NAME ROOM OR ACCT. NO.

NCR TRADE MARK B-6758 OPERATOR

FIGURE 2.7. TELEPHONE CHARGE VOUCHER USED AS AUTHORITY FOR THE FRONT OFFICE CASHIER TO POST TELEPHONE CHARGE TO GUEST BILL.

the room rack slips. The night clerk prepares a room revenue report. It is audited by the night auditor, and the information from it is transferred to the summary sales journal.

Income from the telephone department is recorded on telephone vouchers and the telephone traffic sheet. The telephone vouchers are the

VOUCHER NUMBER	NAME OF PARTY CALLING	ROOM NUMBER	PLACE CALLED	DISTRIBUTION			TOTAL	
				PHONE CO'S CHARGE	TAX	OUR SERVICE CHARGE	HOUSE CALLS	GUEST CHARGES
9704	J. Macey	103	Boston	70	07	20		97
9705	P. Jarvis	216	Albany	1 50	15	20		1 85
	R. Hunt (Manager)		Stanford	60	06		66	
9706	B. Buchner	208	Trenton	2 10	21	20		2 51
9707	J. Macey	103	Worchester	1 40	14	20		1 74
9708	L. Ellis	104	Bridgewater	60	06	20		86
9709	R. Nappi	210	Port Washington	20	03	20		43
9710	G. Grace	215	Monticello	1 00	10	20		1 30
9711	B. Hardinburgh	201	Albany	75	08	20		1 03
				8 85	90	1 60		10 69
				8 85				10 69
				90				66
				1 60				11 35
				11 35				

FIGURE 2.8. THE TELEPHONE TRAFFIC SHEET.

	Date	Day	Room sales	Food Sales		
				Dining room	Bar	Total food
1	June 1	Monday	633 –	180 80	7 –	187
2	2	Tuesday	650 –	220 –	21 –	241
3	3	Wednesday	655 –	350 50	25 –	375
4			1938 –	751 30	53 –	804
5						751 30
6						804 30
7						
8			Credit			Credit
9			Room Sales			Food Sales
10			#401			#410
11						
12						
13						
14						

SHEET NO. _____   NAME Accounts Receivable   ACCOUNT NO. 103
TERMS
RATING   ADDRESS
CREDIT LIMIT

DATE 19	ITEMS	FOLIO	/	DEBITS	DATE 19	ITEMS	FOLIO	/	CREDITS
June 30		SSJ		2673 30					

SHEET NO. _____   NAME Sales Taxes Payable   ACCOUNT NO. 226
TERMS
RATING   ADDRESS
CREDIT LIMIT

DATE 19	ITEMS	FOLIO	/	DEBITS	DATE 19	ITEMS	FOLIO	/	CREDITS
					June 30		SSJ		1540 01

FIGURE 2.9.   THE SUMMARY SALES JOURNAL AND POSTINGS FROM IT TO LEDGER ACCOUNTS.

	5 Beverage dining room	6 Sales Bar	7 Total beverage	8 Telephone sales	9 Sales tax	10 Grand total	11 Cash sales	12 Accounts receivable	
	93 25	35 15	68 40	10 69	4 51	944 40	170 86	773 54	1
	63 —	70 —	133 —	18 60	51 20	1093 80	230 14	863 66	2
	52 —	83 50	135 50	22 30	58 30	1246 60	210 50	1036 10	3
	148 25	188 65	336 90	51 59	154 01	3284 80	611 50	2673 30	4
		148 25						611 50	5
		336 90						3284 80	6
									7
			Credit	Credit	Credit		Debit	Debit	8
			Beverage	Telephone	Sales Tax		Exchange	Accounts	9
			Sales	Sales	Payable		#601	Receivable	10
			#421	#930	#226			#103	11
									12
									13
									14
									15

SHEET NO. _____   ACCOUNT NO. 401

TERMS   NAME   Room Sales

RATING   ADDRESS

CREDIT LIMIT

DATE 19	ITEMS	FOLIO	/	DEBITS	DATE 19	ITEMS	FOLIO	/	CREDITS
					June 30		SJ		1938 —

SHEET NO. _____   ACCOUNT NO. 410

TERMS   NAME   Food Sales

RATING   ADDRESS

CREDIT LIMIT

DATE 19	ITEMS	FOLIO	/	DEBITS	DATE 19	ITEMS	FOLIO	/	CREDITS
					June 30		SJ		8049 30

FIGURE 2.9. (Continued.)

cashier's authorization to post a telephone charge to a guest bill. The vouchers and telephone traffic sheet are audited by the night auditor and used as a basis for posting telephone income to the summary sales journal.

Income from other departments of the hotel is also recorded on similar sales journals, audited by the night auditor, and posted to the summary sales journal.

QUESTIONS FOR DISCUSSION

1. Explain the purposes of subsidiary journals and how they achieve the desired results.
2. The author has stressed the importance of posting all charges to guest bills as soon as they are incurred. If we have addresses for all guests, why is it difficult to collect for charges once the guest leaves the hotel?

3. If all restaurant checks are accounted for by the restaurant cashier, is it still possible that someone could get a meal without the cashier knowing about it?

4. Sales tax for telephone sales is not kept separate when posting to guest bills, but is included in telephone sales; nor is sales tax separated when the total of telephone traffic sheet is posted to the summary sales journal. Why?

5. Only telephone calls charged to guests are recorded as sales. Why don't we also include house calls?

6. Why is the sales tax column of the summary sales journal posted to a liability account instead of an income account in the general ledger?

3 | Accounting for Cash Receipts

You will recall that the cash ledger account in your basic accounting work became congested with figures after only a few transactions. For that reason, a special journal has been set up to deal with cash received and another to deal with cash paid out. Our purpose in setting up these two journals remains the same as in the previous chapter. We will try to keep clutter out of the ledger accounts, yet retain enough detail in our records so that we can get specific information if we so desire. The records pertaining to cash receipts will be discussed in this chapter. We will reserve our discussion of cash paid out for a later chapter.

THE FRONT OFFICE CASH SHEET

Money received from guests is first recorded on the *front office cash sheet* (Figure 3.1). We have already seen how money received as a result of cash sales in the various departments is turned over to the front office cashier and recorded on her front office cash sheet. She will also receive money from guests paying their bills, from people sending money in as advance deposits on rooms, and other people paying money to the hotel. All this is recorded as illustrated in Figure 3.1. Receipts from guest checking out or from advance deposits are recorded in the "guests" column of the front office cash sheet.

The front office cashier will also give out small amounts of money for guests. Gratuities that the guests charge to their accounts will be given to employees out of the funds of the front office cashier's bank, as well as any other money for such things as collect packages, services performed by outside firms for guests, and the like. These disbursements are recorded on the right-hand portion of the cash sheet.

47

Front Office Cashier's Receipts and Disbursements

No. 1

DATE June 1, 19___ CASHIER Mary WATCH 8:00 A.M. 4:00 P.M.

WM. ALLEN & CO., N.Y. STOCK FORM 8122

ROOM NO.	ACCT NO.	NAME	✓	RECEIPTS — GUESTS	RECEIPTS — OTHER	ROOM NO.	ACCT NO.	NAME	✓	DISBURSEMENTS — DETAIL	DISBURSEMENTS — GUESTS	DISBURSEMENTS — HOUSE
		Cash sales Dept.				203	10748	Sunshine		Tips	2 —	
		Food 115.80				210	10748	Pepper		Flowers	5 —	
		Liquor 17.25				108	10758	Carole		COD	3.75	
		Tax 6.66			139 71					Total	10.75	
		Cash Sales Bar										
		Food —										
		Liquor 29.65										
		Tax 1.50			31 15							
					170 86							
205	10763	Beverly		27 50								
111	10752	Steller		75 80								
112	10753	Reasons		56 30								
218	10760	James		105 20								
		Total Guests		264 80								
		Cash Sales		170 86								
		Total Receipts		435 66								

RECAPITULATION

TOTAL RECEIPTS	435 66
DISBURSEMENTS—GUESTS	10 75
DISBURSEMENTS—HOUSE	
TOTAL DISBURSEMENTS	
DEPOSIT	424 91

FIGURE 3.1. FRONT OFFICE CASH SHEET.

The cashier will add all columns at the conclusion of her watch and summarize the information at the bottom of the cash sheet under "recapitulation." She will verify that her cash drawer balances with the information on her cash sheet. Her opening bank plus the total deposit should equal the amount in her cash drawer. Her deposit will be put in a deposit envelope and turned in to the accounting department for verification and deposit into the hotel's bank account. The cash sheet will be audited by the night auditor and the day auditor.

Cashiers sometimes make mistakes in handling cash, although professional cashiers are surprisingly accurate. They pride themselves on their accuracy and often perform their duties for several days without making any error in cash. When a mistake is made, it will show up when the cashier balances her cash at the conclusion of her watch. Her cash drawer will be over or short the required deposit. Hotels have different ways of handling this situation. Some require that the cashier turn in

CASH REPORT

CLASSIFICATION	DATE	TRANS. SYMBOLS	NET TOTALS	CORRECTIONS	MACH. TOTALS	
PAID						
CLOSING	JUN-1? PAID					
OPENING	JUN-1? PAID				★ 435.66X★	
					★ .00X	
CASH RECEIVED					435.66	
PAID OUT						
CLOSING	JUN-1? PD.OUT					
OPENING·	JUN-1? PD.OUT				★ 10.75X	
					★ .00X	
CASH PAID OUT					10.75	
NET CASH					424.91	

ON DUTY 8:00 AM

OFF DUTY 4:00 PM

CASHIER

Mary

WILLIAM ALLEN & CO., N.Y., STOCK FORM 4200

FIGURE 3.2.   CASH REPORT FORM USING THE NCR 4200.

Roger Young's
Summary Cash

Date	Day	Cash sales	Accounts receivable	Sundries amount	explanation
June 1	Monday	170 86	264 80		
2	Tuesday	230 14	560 28		
3	Wednesday	210 50	340 80		
		611 50	1165 88		
		611 50			
		1165 88			
		1777 38			
		Credit to	Credit to		
		exchange	accounts		
		#601	receivable		
			#103		

FIGURE 3.3.   CASH RECEIPTS JOURNAL.

the proper deposit, leaving her cash drawer over or short the normal amount. These hotels adjust cash drawers periodically. Other hotels adjust cash drawers daily and require the cashier to turn in only that amount that would leave her with her normal bank. The former method requires less bookkeeping than the latter, but it does not provide the accurate control of cash sometimes desired.

The Front Office Cash Sheet When Posting Machines Are Used

Most hotels now use a posting machine to record charges to guest bills, as well as cash received or paid out. Bookkeeping using a machine is not very different from using the hand front office cashier's sheet. As revenue is received, it is recorded on the appropriate guest bill. As cash is paid out, an appropriate voucher is completed, and the amount paid

5 Total receipts	6 Advances to guests	7 Net receipts	8	9	10	11	12	
435 66	10 75	424 91						1
790 42	20 30	770 12						2
551 30	7 30	544						3
1 777 38	38 35	1 739 03						4
								5
		1 739 03						6
		38 35						7
		1 777 38						8
	Debit to accounts receivable #103	Debit to cash #100						12

out is recorded to the guest bill. When the cashier comes on duty, she records the opening balances with the cash-received and cash-paid-out keys of her machine. At the conclusion of her watch, she again takes totals of these two keys. The difference between the opening and closing totals in these keys is the amount she will be responsible for turning in. Needless to say, each cashier is assigned her own cash-received key and cash-paid-out key. Figure 3.2 illustrates the cash report when the NCR 4200 is used.

THE CASH RECEIPTS JOURNAL

Information from the front office cash sheets of all of the cashiers is audited and summarized by the chief cashier and posted to the cash receipts journal (Figure 3.3). One line of the journal is used for each day's receipts. The journal is totaled each month, and the columns are posted (Figure 3.4) to general ledger accounts.

It is posted as follows. The cash sales column will total the same amount as the cash sales column in our summary sales journal. You will recall that the column was posted as a *debit* to exchange from the summary sales journal. This same figure from the cash receipts journal is posted as a *credit* to exchange. The exchange account is a wash account; that is, equal debits and credits are always posted to it.

You might ask why we would set up a ledger account for an apparently useless purpose. The answer is that we always want to post equal debits and credits from each journal. Further, if we were to post

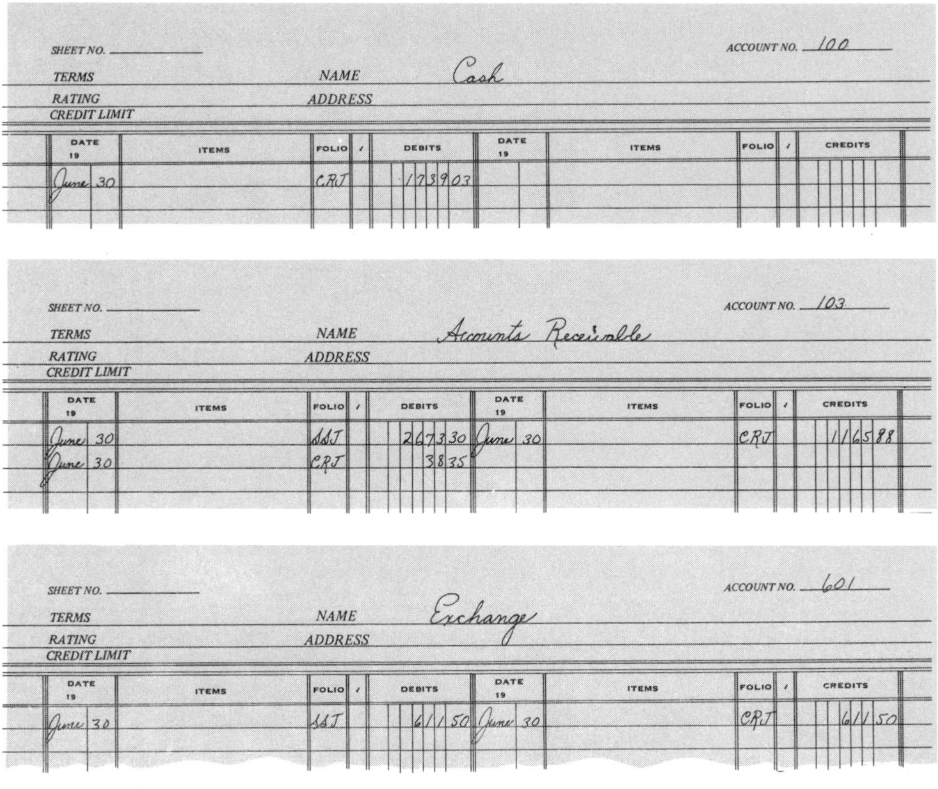

SHEET NO. ACCOUNT NO. 100
TERMS NAME Cash
RATING ADDRESS
CREDIT LIMIT

DATE 19	ITEMS	FOLIO	✓	DEBITS	DATE 19	ITEMS	FOLIO	✓	CREDITS
June 30		CRJ		1739 03					

SHEET NO. ACCOUNT NO. 103
TERMS NAME Accounts Receivable
RATING ADDRESS
CREDIT LIMIT

DATE 19	ITEMS	FOLIO	✓	DEBITS	DATE 19	ITEMS	FOLIO	✓	CREDITS
June 30		SSJ		2673 30	June 30		CRJ		1165 88
June 30		CRJ		38 35					

SHEET NO. ACCOUNT NO. 601
TERMS NAME Exchange
RATING ADDRESS
CREDIT LIMIT

DATE 19	ITEMS	FOLIO	✓	DEBITS	DATE 19	ITEMS	FOLIO	✓	CREDITS
June 30		SSJ		611 50	June 30		CRJ		611 50

FIGURE 3.4. LEDGER ACCOUNTS FROM CASH RECEIPTS JOURNAL.

the cash sales column from the summary sales journal as a debit to cash and also post the correct cash amount as a debit to cash from the cash receipts journal, we would be posting more cash than we should to our cash ledger account. In effect, the cash sales would be posted twice. One solution to this problem is to eliminate cash sales from the cash receipts journal entirely. In this fashion we could post the cash sales from the summary sales journal and the rest of the receipts from the cash receipts journal. However, most accountants do not do it that way but prefer to set up the exchange account. Further, if we eliminated cash sales from the cash receipts journal, the front office cashier would not post cash receipts to her front office cash sheet, and the night auditor could not do a proper audit on cash.

The accounts receivable column is posted as a credit to accounts receivable (since we are reducing the amount that is owed us and we always show a reduction in an asset by a credit entry). The sundries column is used for other cash receipts that we might have, such as bank loans or new investment in the business. Whatever account is involved would be credited individually from this column.

The advances-to-guest column represents cash disbursements by the front office cashier on behalf of guests. It would be posted as a debit to

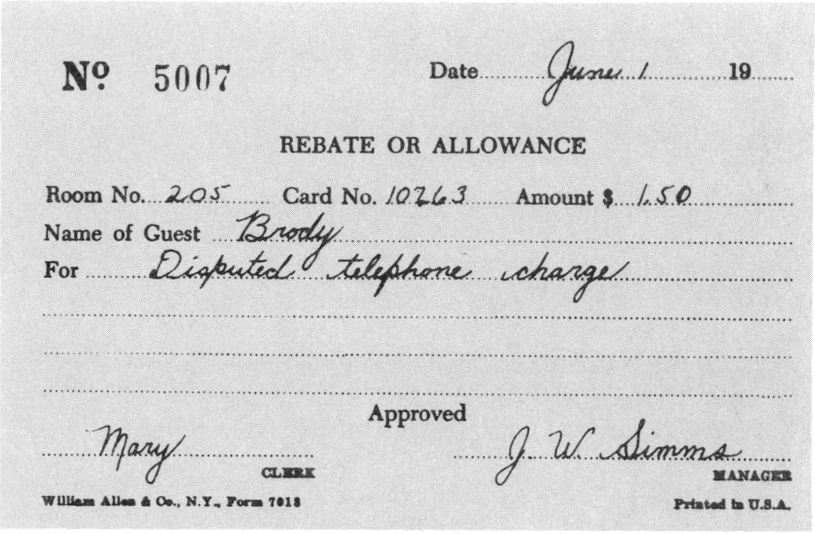

Nº 5007 Date June 1 19

REBATE OR ALLOWANCE

Room No. 205 Card No. 10263 Amount $ 1.50

Name of Guest Brody

For Disputed telephone charge

Approved

Mary CLERK

J. W. Simms MANAGER

William Allen & Co., N.Y., Form 7018

Printed in U.S.A.

FIGURE 3.5. ALLOWANCE VOUCHER.

Roger Young's Allowance

	Date	Name	1. Room no.	2. Account no	3. Total	4. Rooms
1	June 1	Brody	205	10763	1 50	
2	1	Pearsons	112	10753	2 10	2
3	1	Barr	211	10754	3 15	
4	1	Smith	102	10783	26 25	25
5	1	Craig	106	10741	2 10	
6					35 10	27
7						
8						27
9						5
10						1
11						
12					35 10	35
13						
14					Credit to	Debit
15					accounts	room
16					receivable	allowance
17					#103	#402
18						
19						
20						

FIGURE 3.6. ALLOWANCE JOURNAL.

accounts receivable, since we are charging our guests for the amount we disbursed for them.

Finally, the net receipts column would be posted as a debit to cash; and it represents all the cash we took in including cash sales, cash our guests paid on their accounts, and other cash we received.

THE ALLOWANCE JOURNAL

Many guests who check out of the hotel challenge charges put on their bill. They forget about phone calls they made, complain about

Hotel
Journal

5 Food	6 Telephone	7 Sales tax	8 Sundries	9 Detail	10	11	12	
	1 50							1
			10					2
3 -			15					3
			1 25					4
2 -			10					5
5 -	1 50		1 60					6
								7
								8
								9
								10
								11
								12
								13
Debit to food allowance #411	Debit to telephone allowance #431	Debit to sales tax payable #226						14–18

being overcharged for their room, or in some other fashion object to
paying for part of the charges. Sometimes the hotel makes a mistake. It
is possible to post a charge to the wrong account and have the error
go undetected until the guest checks out. Sometimes the manager gives
complimentary rooms to special guests after a charge has been made
for the room. For whatever reason, when the hotel agrees to give credit
for charges on a guest bill, it is necessary that an allowance voucher
(Figure 3.5) be prepared and signed by the department manager. The
guest is given proper credit on his bill and the voucher is posted to the
allowance journal (Figure 3.6).

SHEET NO. _____

TERMS										
RATING			**NAME** Accounts Receivable						**ACCOUNT NO.** 103	
CREDIT LIMIT			**ADDRESS**							

DATE 19	ITEMS	FOLIO	✓	DEBITS	DATE 19	ITEMS	FOLIO	✓	CREDITS
June 30		S S J		2 6 7 3 30	June 30		C R J		1 1 6 5 88
June 30		C R J		3 8 35	June 30		A J		3 5 10

SHEET NO. _____

TERMS										
RATING			**NAME** Sales Tax Payable						**ACCOUNT NO.** 226	
CREDIT LIMIT			**ADDRESS**							

DATE 19	ITEMS	FOLIO	✓	DEBITS	DATE 19	ITEMS	FOLIO	✓	CREDITS
June 30		A J		1 60	June 30		S J		1 54 01

SHEET NO. _____

TERMS										
RATING			**NAME** Room Allowance						**ACCOUNT NO.** 402	
CREDIT LIMIT			**ADDRESS**							

DATE 19	ITEMS	FOLIO	✓	DEBITS	DATE 19	ITEMS	FOLIO	✓	CREDITS
June 30		A J		27 —					

SHEET NO. _____

TERMS										
RATING			**NAME** Food Allowance						**ACCOUNT NO.** 411	
CREDIT LIMIT			**ADDRESS**							

DATE 19	ITEMS	FOLIO	✓	DEBITS	DATE 19	ITEMS	FOLIO	✓	CREDITS
June 30		A J		5 —					

SHEET NO. _____

TERMS										
RATING			**NAME** Telephone Allowance						**ACCOUNT NO.** 431	
CREDIT LIMIT			**ADDRESS**							

DATE 19	ITEMS	FOLIO	✓	DEBITS	DATE 19	ITEMS	FOLIO	✓	CREDITS
June 30		A J		1 50					

FIGURE 3.7.   LEDGER ACCOUNTS FROM ALLOWANCE JOURNAL.

Our books are set up in such a fashion that we have already credited an income account and debited accounts receivable in the summary sales journal for the charge. We now need a procedure to reverse that action, and the allowance journal does it very nicely. In effect, we are saying that we charged too much to accounts receivable and credited too much to sales.

The allowance journal is balanced in the usual fashion and is posted as follows. The total column is posted as a credit to accounts receivable, since we want to show a decrease in the amount owed to us. The remaining columns (Figure 3.7) are posted as debits. The rooms column is posted as a debit to room allowance (an income account), the food column is posted as a debit to food allowance (an income account), the telephone column is posted as a debit to telephone allowance (an income account), the sales tax column is posted as a debit to sales tax payable (a liability account), and entries in the sundries column are posted as debits to the specific accounts involved.

RECAPPING OUR WORK

Let us pause for a moment to summarize our work to this point. The system of keeping accounting records developed in Chapter 1 was fine for a hotel with only a very few transactions. However, all hotels have large numbers of transactions and would not be able to use the system as originally laid out. It was necessary for us to modify our accounting system to keep clutter out of the ledger. So we created a series of special journals to take care of those transactions that occur frequently. The summary sales journal summarized all those transactions dealing with sales, the cash receipts journal summarized all our cash received, the allowance journal summarized allowances to guest bills. Figure 3.8 diagramatically represents our new system as we have developed it thus far.

THE NIGHT AUDIT

Our discussion has vaguely made reference to the night audit and the transcript. It is now time to go into the work of the night auditor and to show the part he plays in our bookkeeping system.

The night auditor does his work between the hours of midnight and 8 AM, when the hotel is quietest and when most of the revenue has been charged to the various departments. He has the important job of verifying all the work of the front office and other sales departments with respect to guest charges and cash. His primary jobs are to ascer-

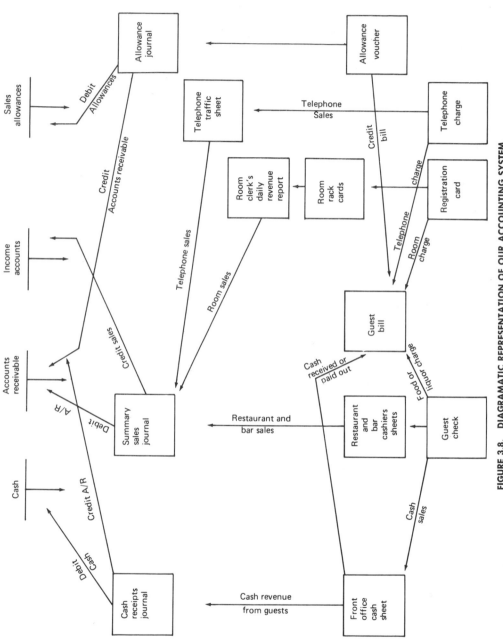

FIGURE 3.8.   DIAGRAMATIC REPRESENTATION OF OUR ACCOUNTING SYSTEM.

tain that all charges posted to guest bills were done so correctly, that all room revenue is posted, and that all cash is properly accounted for. In the process of doing his work he will also verify that all revenue is accounted for. He will act as a double check on our bookkeeping system.

The night auditor starts his work by separating all vouchers into their respective departments and verifying that the totals of each department's vouchers agree with the departmental sales journals. This means that the total restaurant guest checks must equal the total on the restaurant cashier's sheet, the total of the bar guest checks must equal the total on the bar cashier's sheet, the total telephone vouchers must equal the total of the telephone traffic sheet, and the total allowance vouchers must equal the total of the allowance journal. If one or more vouchers is missing, the night auditor makes a duplicate and charges the appropriate guest bill with the amount.

He then takes all the guest bills from the cashier's department and enters the information contained on the guest bills for the day on the *transcript of guest ledger* (Figure 3.9). As he does his work he will also post the room charge on each bill and add it up, carrying totals forward to the next day. The information from each bill is put on a separate line on the transcript. Room number, folio number, name, opening balance (if any), room charge, and so on are written in the columns provided.

The transcript is then added, and the auditor verifies that all charges have been put on the bills and transcript correctly. If the totals of the various charge columns on the transcript agree with the departmental sales totals, he is reasonably certain that charges are posted to guest bills correctly. There is a possibility that a charge was posted to the wrong account, an error that might never be caught. In Figure 3.9 the total restaurant column agrees with the sum of restaurant sales in the dining room and bar; the total bar column agrees with the total bar sales in the restaurant and bar; the total telephone column agrees with the total guest charges on the telephone traffic sheet; and the total room sales agrees with the total sales as reported on the room clerk's daily revenue report.

The night auditor verifies that all guest bills have been accounted for by (1) comparing last night's closing balance of guest bills with the opening balance on tonight's transcript and (2) verifying that the house count and room count on the transcript agree with the night clerk's daily revenue report.

He then verifies that the total charges for the day have been added correctly on all the bills. This verification is made by comparing the

ROOM NUMBER	NO. PERS.	CARD NUMBER	NAME	BALANCE AT BEGINNING OF DAY		ROOM	TAX	REST.	BEVER-AGES	PHON
				DEBIT	CREDIT					
c/o		10763	Brody	29						
c/o		10752	Hibber	75 80						
c/o		10753	Pearsons	58 40						
c/o		10760	James	105 20						
c/o		10754	Barr	66 15						
c/o		10783	Smith	26 25						
c/o		10741	Craig	84 60						
100	3	10770	Blum			30 -	1 50			
103	2	10784	J. Macey	32 -		25 -	1 25 / 23	3 00	1 50	17 9
104	2	10771	Ellis			25 -	1 25			8
105	2	10750	Pott	26 25		25 -	1 25			
108	2	10758	Goulel			25 -	1 25 / 89	28 50	9 2 -	
110	1	10757	Roberts			20 -	10 / 1 00			
111	2	10742	Reiger	23 10		22 -	1 10			
114	2	10756	Katin			22 -	1 10			
115	3	10749	Glickman	36 20		30 -	08 / 1 50	17 50	4 -	
116	2	10769	Coody			22 -	1 10			
118	2	10743	T. Grace	64 80		22 -	30 / 1 10	4 -	2 -	
119	2	10751	Pratt			22 -	1 10			
201	2	10782	Hardenbergh			25 -	1 25			1 0
203	2	10748	Sunshine	50 50		25 -	75 / 1 25	13 -	2 -	
204	2	10755	Barry			25 -	35 / 1 25	6 -	1 -	
205	3	10745	Shapiro			30 -	1 50			
206	1	10767	Briggs			20 -	1 00			
208	2	10759	Buchner	26 25		25 -	1 25			25
210	2	10768	Nappi	76 30		25 -	1 25			4
211	2	10744	Jones	23 10		22 -	1 10			
212	3	10772	Grant	31 50		30 -	1 50			
215	2	10766	St Grace	28		22 -	1 10			1 3
216	1	10785	Jarvis			20 -	1 00			1 8
217	2	10746	Oskanos	23 10		22 -	1 10			
218	2	10780	Schreiver	46 20		22 -	1 10			
219	3	10747	Jessenholtz			30 -	1 50			
			City Ledger							
			Cash Sales				8 16	115 80	46 90	
26	54			932 70		633 -	44 51	187 80	68 40	10 6

FIGURE 3.9.   TRANSCRIPT OF GUEST LEDGER.

LEG.	LAUNDRY	VALET	BAGG.			CASH DISBR.	TRANS.	TOTAL CHARGES	CREDITS			BALANCE AT END OF DAY	
									CASH	ALLOW.	TRANS	DEBIT	CREDIT
									27 50	1 50			
									75 80				
									56 30	2 10			
									105 20				
										3 15	63 —		
										26 25		To American Express	
										2 10	82 50	Complimentary Room	
								31 50				To C/L	31 50
								33 69					65 69
								27 11					27 11
								26 25					52 50
							3 75	71 49					71 49
								21 —					21 —
								23 10					46 20
								23 10					23 10
								54 08					90 28
								23 10					23 10
								29 40					94 20
								23 10					23 10
								27 28					27 28
							2 00	44 00					94 50
								33 60					33 60
								31 50					31 50
								21 —					21 —
								28 76					55 01
							5 00	31 68					107 98
								23 10					46 20
								31 50					63 —
								24 40					52 40
								22 85					22 85
								23 10					46 20
								23 10					69 30
								31 50					31 50
							145 50	145 50					145 50
								170 86	170 86				
						10 75	145 50	1100 65	435 66	35 10	145 50		1417 09

Proof of charges:
6 33
44 51
187 70
68 40
10 69
10 75
145 50
1100 65

932 70
+ 1100 65
————
2033 35
− 616 26
————
1417 09
} Balance

Sum of credits:
435 66
− 35 10
145 50
616 26

total charges column with the sum of all the individual charge columns. On our transcript, the total charges column agrees with the sum of the room, bar, restaurant, phone, sales tax, debit transfer, and cash disbursements columns. The above procedure proves that all charges have been added correctly on all bills, because if there were errors, the total charges column would not agree with the sum of the individual charge columns. Can you determine why?

His next job is to verify that all cash is accounted for. He compares the front office cash sheets with the cash receipts and cash disbursements columns on the transcript. If a guest bill should show cash being paid and that amount does not appear on one of the front office cash sheets, then there is missing money, a situation that can be quite serious.

The allowance column is verified with the allowance journal. It is important that the night auditor checks to be certain proper authorization was given for all allowances. He must determine that the signatures on all allowance vouchers are genuine and that only authorized persons signed them.

The transfer column is checked to be certain that all transfer credits equal all transfer debits. These columns are used to show that amounts are transferred from one guest account to another; thus, when we transfer *credit* a guest bill we must transfer *debit* another bill for the same amount. We will discuss this concept more fully in the next section.

The transcript is then balanced. The formula for balancing is as follows:

Opening balance + total charges — credits = balance at the end of day

In Figure 3.9 the opening balance is $932.70, the sum of the total charges is $1,100.65, the sum of the credits is $616.26, and therefore the balance at the end of the day is $1,417.09. We are now reasonably certain that all guest bills are accurate because if there were errors in one or more guest bills, the transcript would not balance according to the above formula. Can you determine why?

City Ledger and Transfers

We have conspicuously avoided any reference to city ledger accounts because we wanted to keep our work as uncomplicated as possible. We will not make it a part of our accounting system, but we would be remiss in our duty if we did not explain it.

The term "city ledger" refers to all those accounts receivable for which there are balances but which are not for hotel guests. This category of accounts includes all persons who were guests and who did not pay upon leaving (perhaps the hotel agreed to send them the bill or they were skippers), those persons or businesses in the community that have credit privileges at the hotel, all credit card accounts, and anyone else who owes the hotel money on open account and is not a guest in the hotel at the time. Those accounts for people presently residing in the hotel are referred to as active accounts. All our accounts, active and city ledger, are accounts receivable. We will not distinguish between them in our accounting system except on the transcript. The active accounts are the guest folios and are located in the cashier's department. The city ledger accounts are also of the same form, but are located in the accounting department of most hotels.

When an active account goes into city ledger, it is transferred on the transcript using the debit and credit transfer columns. We carry the total city ledger balance on our transcript but do not carry the individual accounts because of their large numbers and because they are often inactive. We carry on our transcript only those accounts we deal with often.

The transfer column on the transcript can also be used to transfer amounts between one active guest account and another. For example, if the guest in room 112 decided he wanted to absorb the charges for the guest in room 111, the debit and credit transfer columns would be used for this purpose. Or if we posted a charge to the wrong account and did not discover it until the guest was checking out, we might transfer it to the correct account at that time.

The Night Audit Using a Posting Machine

The same basic principles of auditing and the same information as appeared on the hand transcript carry over into the posting machines. If you understand the night audit using the hand transcript, the night audit on any posting machine will be simple once you learn how to operate the machine. It is not our intention to go into detail about the operation of any of the machines in use. What is important now is that you understand that the information from the machine is similar to the hand transcript and that the night auditor will do essentially the same work and go through the same procedures as with the hand transcript (Figure 3.10).

The Significance of the Night Audit

It should be obvious that the night audit is of considerable help to the bookkeeping department in verifying revenue totals and cash totals.

D—NIGHT AUDITOR'S MACHINE BALANCE NO._____

DATE _____

DEPARTMENT	DATE	DESCRIPTION	NET TOTALS	CORRECTIONS	MACHINE TOTALS	
ROOM	JUN-12	ROOM			★ 633.00X✻	
TAX	JUN-12	TAX			★ 44.51X✻	
TELEPHONE	JUN-12	PHONE			★ .00X✻	
LONG DISTANCE	JUN-12	LDIST			★ 10.69X✻	
LAUNDRY	JUN-12	LNDRY			★ .00X✻	
VALET	JUN-12	VALET			★ .00X✻	
GARAGE	JUN-12	G'RAGE			★ .00X✻	
TELEGRAM	JUN-12	TELGM			★ .00X✻	
BEVERAGE	JUN-12	BEVGE			★ 68.40X✻	
MISCELLANEOUS	JUN-12	MISC			★ .00X✻	
RESTAURANT	JUN-12	RESTR			★ 187.80X✻	
TRANSFER CHARGE	JUN-12	TR.CH.			★ 145.50X✻	
PAID OUT	JUN-12	PD.OUT			★ 10.75X✻	
TOTAL DEBITS					*1100.65*	
TRANSFER CREDIT	JUN-12	TR.CR.			★ 145.50X	
ADJUSTMENT	JUN-12	ADJ			★ 35.10X	
PAID	JUN-12	PAID			★ 435.66X	
TOTAL CREDITS					*616.26*	
NET DIFFERENCE					*484.39*	
OPENING DR BALANCE					*932.70*	
NET OUTSTANDING					*1417.09*	
TOTAL MCH. DR. BALANCE	JUN-12				★ 1,417.09X	
TOTAL MCH. CR BALANCE	JUN-12	IN.CR.			★ .00X✻	
NET OUTSTANDING						
CORRECTIONS						

DETECTOR COUNTER READINGS: ☐ DATE CHANGED

AUDITOR'S CONTROL_____ ☐ CONTROL TOTALS AT ZERO

MACH. NUMBER_____ ☐ MASTER TAPE LOCKED   **AUDITOR**

☐ AUDIT CONTROL LOCKED

WILLIAM ALLEN & CO., N. Y., STOCK FORM 4202-L.

FIGURE 3.10.   "D" CARD SHOWING NIGHT AUDIT USING NCR 4200.

The totals on the transcript must equal the totals on the departmental revenue records; and these totals must equal the totals posted to the summary sales journals, cash receipts journal, and allowance journal. In addition, the transcript provides us with the composition of our accounts receivable at any time by verifying it with the amount shown on the transcript. The accounts receivable account in the general ledger is really a *control* account, and the actual ledger accounts are the active guest folios and the city ledger guest folios. Periodically we will want to verify that the control total agrees with the total of the actual accounts.

The night audit is an essential part of our accounting system. If we did not have it, we would not know if our accounts receivable control total was correct, and we would not be sure guest charges were properly posted to guest accounts or that guest accounts were properly added.

SUMMARY

Special journals for the receipt and disbursement of cash are necessary because of the many transactions affecting our cash ledger account. This chapter has dealt with these special journals needed for the receipt of cash.

All money received from guests is first recorded on the front office cash sheet, including receipt of cash sales, advance deposits, and other miscellaneous cash from guests. Cash paid out of the cashier's bank on behalf of guests is recorded on the right-hand portion of the front office cash sheet. The cashier adds her front office cash sheet at the conclusion of her watch and verifies its total with the amount of money in her cash drawer. The front office cash sheets from all cashiers are summarized by the chief cashier and posted to the cash receipts journal.

The cash receipts journal is used to record all cash received by the hotel—cash that is received from guests and all other cash received. At the end of the month, the cash receipts journal is totaled and posted to ledger accounts in the general ledger.

The allowance journal is designed to provide a means whereby we can account for credits given to guests for charges already posted to their accounts. The allowance journal reverses the accounting which took place in the summary sales journal. An allowance voucher is prepared, signed by an authorized person in the hotel, and entered in the allowance journal. At the end of the month we total the journal, debit the appropriate income accounts, and credit accounts receivable.

The primary purpose of the night audit is to verify the work of the front office. The night auditor uses a transcript of the guest ledger to perform his work. He records all of the charges and credits to guest accounts on the transcript, totals them, and balances them. He audits all sales records by verifying that the total of all sales vouchers agrees with the total of the sales sheets. The total of the sales sheets must agree with the totals on his transcript of guest ledger. In that fashion, he is able to prove that all sales were recorded to guest accounts or collected as cash. He also verifies that all cash is accounted for and that all guest bills have been accurately added.

Although the night audit is not an integral part of our bookkeeping system, we could not get along without it, because it provides us with a means of verifying the accuracy of our sales records. Further, it provides us with the composition of our accounts receivable. At any time, we can determine the accuracy of our accounts receivable control account by comparing its balance with the balance on the transcript of guest ledger.

QUESTIONS FOR DISCUSSION

1. The front office cash sheet is used to record the receipt of most cash. What cash might not be recorded on the front office cash sheet? Where would it be initially recorded?
2. Why does requiring a cashier to deposit the amount of money listed on her cash sheet as opposed to requiring her to deposit only that amount that will leave her with her normal cash bank provide the hotel with less control over cash?
3. In your own words explain what is meant by the exchange account.
4. The author suggested several types of cash disbursements. Name four other types of cash disbursements the front office cashier might advance money for on behalf of guests.
5. Why is it important that only authorized persons sign allowance vouchers? Who would you authorize to sign them if you were the manager?
6. Would it be possible for the night auditor to do his work at any other time than the midnight to 8 AM shift? Why or why not?
7. Explain why the night auditor is reasonably sure all guest charges were posted correctly. Is it possible he could be wrong?
8. How does the night auditor know that all guest bills are added correctly?
9. Explain why the night audit is an essential part of our bookkeeping system.

4 | Accounting for Purchases

Our accounting system is now able to handle large numbers of transactions pertaining to income and cash received. And certainly the largest volume of transactions occurs in those two areas. However, the hotel will also purchase large quantities of goods each day, and it is desirable to set up a system to deal with them. This chapter will examine how hotels purchase and the resulting bookkeeping techniques.

PURCHASING FOOD AND RELATED ITEMS

The largest amount of money spent by hotels—with the exception of payroll—is on food. It accounts for 20 to 25 percent of the total expenditures of a typical hotel, and the steward or purchasing agent will have the responsibility for ordering these goods. It is very important that (1) the food ordered be only that kind and amount needed, (2) it is purchased at the lowest possible price consistent with the quality desired, (3) only the food ordered is received and we do not receive unwanted merchandise, and (4) we pay only for that amount of food we receive.

To achieve the above objectives our accounting system will have certain controls built into it. The steward and chef will decide on the menu. Usually they must plan for several days in advance. The steward will call up the purveyors he deals with to obtain the current market quotations for the perishable items he wishes to order. The price quoted will be based on the purchase specifications of the hotel. Purchase

Steward's Market Quotation List

On Hand	Article	Wanted	AC	Quotations QX	PD	BL	On Hand	Article	Wanted	Quotations		
	VEAL							POULTRY				
	Breast						25	Chickens, Fryers				
	Brains							Chickens, Roast				
	Feet							Chickens, Broil				
	Fore Quarter							Cocks				
	Hind Quarter							Capons				
	Head							Duck				
	Kidneys							Fowl				
20 lb.	Legs							Geese				
	Liver							Guinea Hens				
	Loins							Guinea Squab				
30 lb.	Racks							Pigeons				
	Saddles											
	Shoulder											
10 lb.	Sweet Breads	10 lb.	(1.10)	1.12		1.15				RD	MO	QV
								SHELL FISH				
								Clams, Chowder				
	LAMB							Clams, Chryst.				
	Breast							Clams, Soft				
36 lb.	Fore Quarter							Crabs, Hard				
	Feet							Crabs, Meat				
	Kidneys							Crabs, Oyster				
	Loins							Crabs, Soft				
15 lb.	Legs	40 lb.	.95	(90)		.95		Lobsters				
	Lamb, Spring						5 lb.	Lobsters, Meat	10 lb.	2.50	(2.40)	2.50
22 lb.	Racks, Double							Lobsters, Tail				
	Racks, Spring							Oysters, Box				
	Saddles							Oysters, Blue Pt.				
	Shoulder							Oysters				
							3 lb.	Scallops	10 lb.	(.80)	.85	.85
							10 lb.	Shrimps	15 lb.	.75	(.70)	.75
	PROVISIONS							Turtle				
15 lb.	Bacon	30 lb.	(60)	.65		.65						
	Bologna							FISH				
	Crepinetter							Bluefish				
5 lb.	Salami	10 lb.	.85	(.80)		.85		Butterfish				
	Hams, Corned							Cod				
	Hams, Fresh							Flounder				
	Hams, Polish							Haddock				
	Hams, Smoked							Halibut				
	Hams, Virginia							Mackerel				
	Pork Loins							Pollock				
8	Link Sausages	15 lb.	(.45)	.50		.50	5 lb.	Pompano	2 lb.	.95	.95	(.90)
20	Frankfurters							Salmon				

FIGURE 4.1. STEWARD'S MARKET QUOTATION LIST.

specifications are the specific requirements of the hotel for each item. For example, the hotel, when ordering ribs of beef, might require U.S. Grade Prime, oven prepared, well trimmed, each seven ribs weighing between 22 and 25 pounds.

The steward will mark down the quoted prices on his *steward's market quotation list* (Figure 4.1). After completing his calls he will circle the lowest price on each item and then return calls to the purveyors to place orders. Normally he will select the lowest priced item, but other considerations, such as dependability of the purveyor and ownership policies, may enter into the decision. A copy of the quotation list will go to the receiving clerk so that he knows what has been ordered, and a copy will go to the accounting department so that they can verify that bills (invoices) are correct.

Sometimes the steward will deal with a salesman who comes to the hotel. In this event, the order must be written up with enough copies to be distributed to the receiving clerk, steward, and accounting department.

Orders for nonperishable items (canned goods) are usually placed by the storeroom clerk on the basis of a par stock. When the inventory of an item depletes to a predetermined par amount, the storeroom clerk automatically reorders. He writes up a purchase requisition (Figure 4.2) in triplicate, sends one copy to the receiving clerk, one to accounting, and retains one copy for his records.

RECEIVING ORDERED GOODS

Normally all goods received by the hotel will be accompanied by an invoice for that order (Figure 4.3). The goods will be received using the following procedure:

1. All goods will be weighed, counted, or otherwise verified to ensure that the amounts received are as ordered and that the invoice shows the proper weights or counts.
2. All goods will be inspected to ensure that the quality of the goods meets or exceeds the purchase specifications of the hotel for each item.
3. Prices will be checked to determine that the amounts charged are the same as those quoted on the steward's market quotation list.
4. All fresh meat will be tagged with a meat tag.
5. The invoice will be stamped with an "invoice stamp," and the clerk will place his initials on the line provided for him.

FIGURE 4.2. PURCHASE REQUISITION.

MAIL ☐ PHONE ☐ VERBAL ☐
RECEIVED BY _____

PURCHASE
ORDER N? - 1156

DATE ____ M ____ J. C. Smart Co. ____ June / 19____

ENTERED BY ____ Bridgeport, Conn. ____

TERMS ____

F.O.B. ____

PLEASE SHIP THE FOLLOWING SUPPLIES

CONDITION GOODS ____ VIA ____ Best Way ____

DEPT. ____

QUANTITY	UNIT	ITEM	PRICE		AMOUNT	
		To – Roger Young's Hotel New York City				
3	cases	# 2½ Tomato puree	7	50	22	50
2	cases	# 10 Whole Tomatoes	9	–	18	–
					$40	50

NO GOODS RECEIVED UNLESS ACCOMPANIED
BY PRICED INVOICE AND THIS ORDER NUMBER

BY ____ J. R. Smith

WILLIAM ALLEN & CO., N.Y. STOCK FORM 6163 PRINTED IN U.S.A.

ALLEN MEATS

NEW YORK CITY

Our Order No. 4120

Customer's Roder No. Phone

Terms Net

Date June 2

Sold To Roger Young's Hotel

QUANTITY	UNIT	ITEM	PRICE	TOTAL
10	LB.	Sweet Breads	$1.10	$11.00
30	LB.	Bacon	.60	18.00
15	LB.	Link Sausage	.45	6.75
				$35.75

FIGURE 4.3. INVOICE.

6. The receiving clerk's daily report form will be filled out showing which items went to stores and which items went to the kitchen for immediate consumption.

The receiving clerk's daily report form is one of our subsidiary journals and is used to initially record the purchase of foods. Figure 4.4 ·illustrates one filled in. The total of the bill is put in the total column, and the items are distributed on the receiving clerk's daily report to stores (inventory) or direct (kitchen). Those items sent to stores will be debited to food inventory and those items sent directly to the kitchen

	Quan.	Unit	Description	Unit price	Amount	Total amount	Purches Food direc
1			Allen Meats				
2	10	lb	Sweet breads	1 10	11 -		
3	30	lb	Bacon	60	18 -		
4	15	lb	Link sausage	45	6 75	35 75	11 -
5							
6			Quick Meats Inc.				
7	40	lb	Lamb legs	90	36 -		
8	10	lb	Salami	80	8 -	44	36 -
9							
10						79 75	$47
11							
12							47 -
13							32 7
14							79 7
15							
16							
17							

FIGURE 4.4. RECEIVING CLERK'S DAILY REPORT.

will be immediately charged to food expense. The sundries column is used for those items received by the receiving clerk that are not food. For example, sometimes the receiving clerk receives items charged to the dining room or housekeeping department.

The clerk will stamp the invoice with the invoice stamp (Figure 4.5) and initial the invoice in the space provided for him. His initials indicate that all goods were received in proper order. The invoice will go to the steward who will note that goods he ordered have been received. The steward will also initial the invoice. The accounting department will get the invoice next. A clerk will verify that it is arithmetically cor-

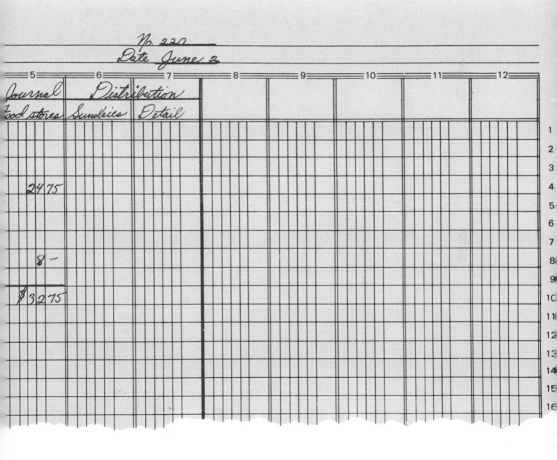

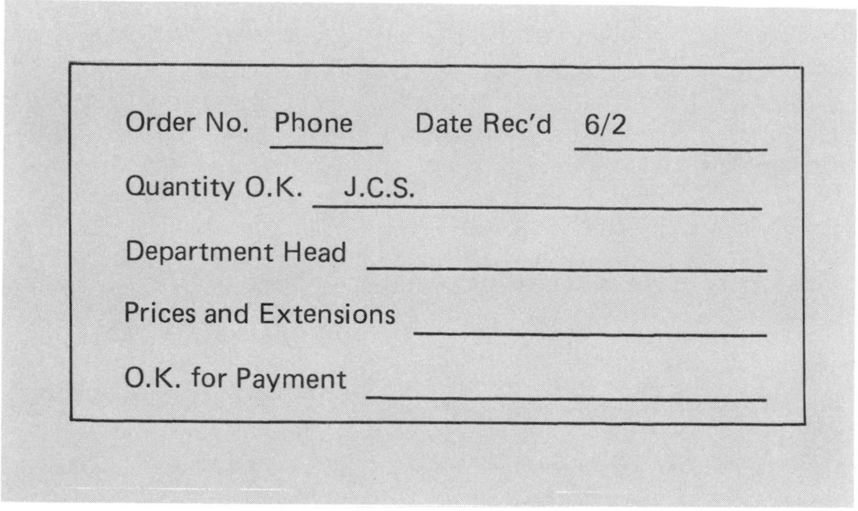

Order No. Phone Date Rec'd 6/2

Quantity O.K. J.C.S.

Department Head

Prices and Extensions

O.K. for Payment

FIGURE 4.5. IMPRESSION OF THE INVOICE STAMP.

rect and compare it with the receiving clerk's daily report. Finally, the invoice will be approved by the manager or his designee for payment.

All fresh meat will be tagged with a meat tag. Fresh meat has a tendency to loose weight while in storage due to loss of moisture. It is, therefore, important that the date of receipt of the meat is put on the tag as well as the correct weight so that shrinkage can be properly accounted for by the food controller (Figure 4.6).

PURCHASING FOR OTHER DEPARTMENTS

Other departments in the hotel will also purchase goods and maintain inventories. The wine steward will be responsible for purchasing all liquor and wine; the housekeeper will buy all housekeeping supplies; and the heads of other departments will purchase the necessary supplies and equipment to keep their departments operating. If an inventory is kept, some form of receiving sheet similar to the receiving clerk's daily report will be kept to inform the accounting department which goods are to be debited to inventory and which goods are to be treated as an expense, as well as to help keep control over purchased items. All invoices will be stamped with the invoice stamp, and each invoice will

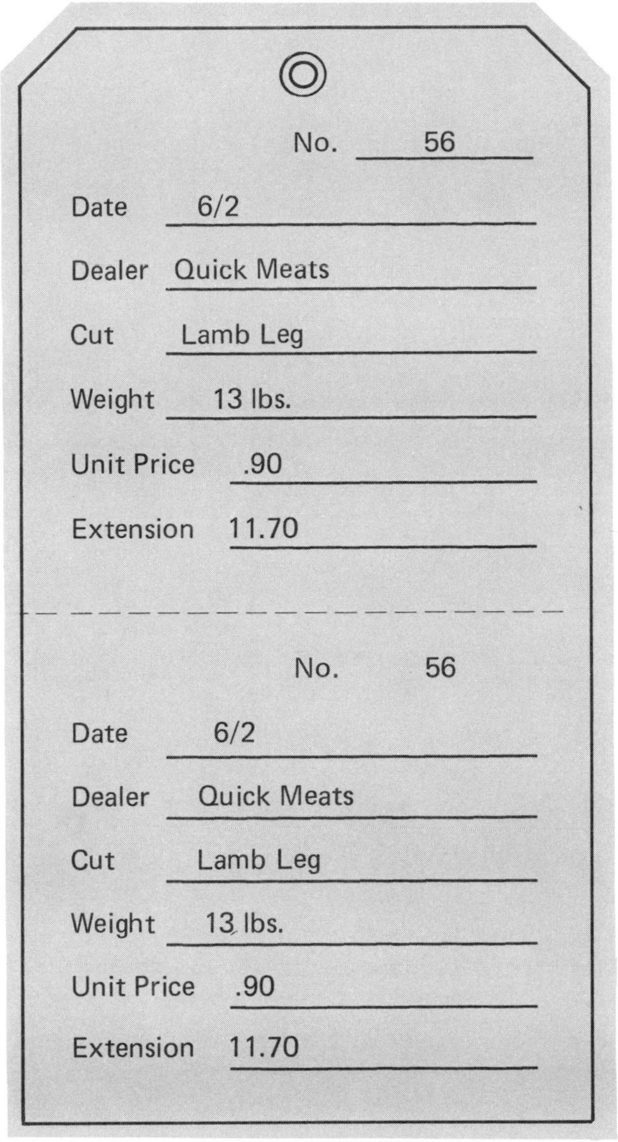

No. _____56_____

Date ___6/2_____

Dealer Quick Meats_____

Cut ___Lamb Leg_____

Weight ___13 lbs._____

Unit Price ___.90_____

Extension ___11.70_____

No. _____56_____

Date ___6/2_____

Dealer ___Quick Meats_____

Cut ___Lamb Leg_____

Weight ___13 lbs._____

Unit Price ___.90_____

Extension ___11.70_____

FIGURE 4.6.   MEAT TAG.

| Date | Creditor | Amount | Purchase Stores | | |
		1	2 Food	3 Liquor	4 Housekeeping
June 2	Allen Meats	35 75	24 75		
2	Quick Meats Inc.	44 —	8 —		
2	Man Repairs	25 —			
3	Shell Fuel Co.	120 —			
3	Janatorial Supply Co.	18 50			70 —
4	New York Light	88 30			
4	Allen Meats	23 70	23 70		
4	Max Repairs	30 —			
		445 25	56 45		70 —
				56 45	
				70 —	
		Credit to	Debit to	47 —	Debit to
		accounts	food	8 50	housekeeping
		payable	inventory	55	supplies
		#204	#121	208 30	inventory
				445 25	#122

FIGURE 4.7. PURCHASE JOURNAL.

follow the same path as our food invoice. The department head will approve it, the accounting department will verify its accuracy and compare it with the receiving sheet, and the manager or his designee will approve the invoice for payment.

THE PURCHASE JOURNAL

Each day the invoices and receiving sheets are turned over to the accounting department to be entered in the purchase journal (Figure

Expenses

5 Food expense	6 Housekeeping expense	7 Repairs and maintenance	8 Heat, light and power	9 Office supplies exp	10 Administrative and general	11 Sundries Detail	12 Amount	
11 —								1
36 —								2
		25 —						3
			120 —					4
	8 50							5
			88 30					6
								7
		30						8
47 —	8 50	55	208 30					9
								10
								11
↓	↓	↓	↓					12
Debit to	Debit to	Debit to	Debit to					13
Food	housekeeping	repairs and	heat, light					14
expense	supplies	maintenance	and power					15
#510	expense	expense	expense					16
	#531	#560	#570					17
								18
								19

4.7). This journal is similar to our summary sales journal. One difference is that each purveyor's shipment or invoice will be entered separately in the journal. The amount is then distributed in the proper column in the journal. We have several columns for inventories and many columns for the most frequent expenses. Any purchase or expense that cannot be categorized in one of the designated columns will be entered in the sundries column along with an explanation of the expense or asset it should be charged to.

The hotel will also receive many invoices by mail. For example, the electric bill will come once each month, as well as other purchases that

SHEET NO. _____								ACCOUNT NO. 121		
TERMS		NAME	Food Inventory							
RATING		ADDRESS								
CREDIT LIMIT										
DATE 19	ITEMS	FOLIO	✓	DEBITS	DATE 19	ITEMS	FOLIO	✓	CREDITS	
June 1	Balance			2350 -						
30		PJ		56 45						

SHEET NO. _____								ACCOUNT NO. 122		
TERMS		NAME	Housekeeping Inventory							
RATING		ADDRESS								
CREDIT LIMIT										
DATE 19	ITEMS	FOLIO	✓	DEBITS	DATE 19	ITEMS	FOLIO	✓	CREDITS	
June 30		PJ		70 -						

SHEET NO. _____								ACCOUNT NO. 204		
TERMS		NAME	Accounts Payable							
RATING		ADDRESS								
CREDIT LIMIT										
DATE 19	ITEMS	FOLIO	✓	DEBITS	DATE 19	ITEMS	FOLIO	✓	CREDITS	
					June 30		PJ		445 25	

SHEET NO. _____								ACCOUNT NO. 510		
TERMS		NAME	Food Expense							
RATING		ADDRESS								
CREDIT LIMIT										
DATE 19	ITEMS	FOLIO	✓	DEBITS	DATE 19	ITEMS	FOLIO	✓	CREDITS	
June 30		PJ		47 -						

SHEET NO. _____								ACCOUNT NO. 531		
TERMS		NAME	Housekeeping Supplies Expense							
RATING		ADDRESS								
CREDIT LIMIT										
DATE 19	ITEMS	FOLIO	✓	DEBITS	DATE 19	ITEMS	FOLIO	✓	CREDITS	
June 30		PJ		8 50						

FIGURE 4.8. LEDGER ACCOUNTS FROM THE PURCHASE JOURNAL.

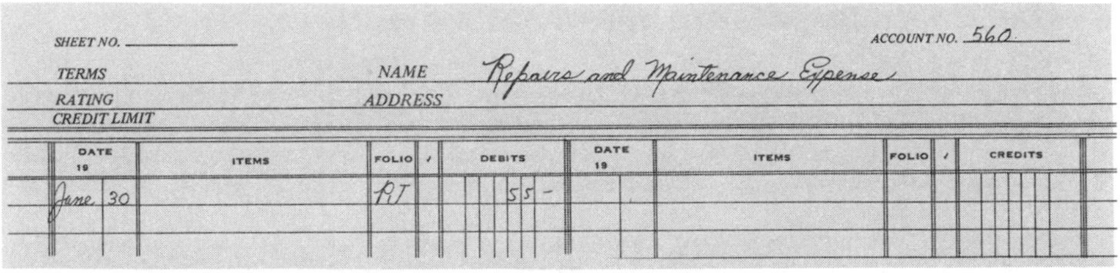

FIGURE 4.8. (Continued.)

are made but not recorded until we receive the bill in the mail. These invoices are entered in the purchase journal, and the appropriate column is debited with the proper amount.

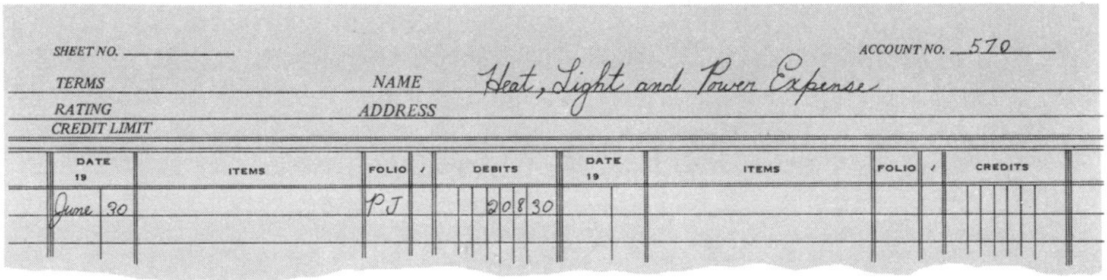

Many miscellaneous purchases are made by personnel of the hotel. Copies of the invoices for such purchases are brought to the accounting department. If these transactions are small in nature and frequently occurring, we will not enter the invoice in the purchase journal but will wait until we receive a monthly statement. For example, we may have a charge account with the local hardware store and buy from them almost daily. The invoices will be put in a file and the total will be entered when the monthly statement arrives. This procedure saves making many entries in our journal when one will suffice.

At the end of the month the purchase journal is totaled and balanced in the same way as our other journals (Figure 4.8). The total of the amount column must equal the total of the rest of the columns. We post to the general ledger accounts as follows. The amount column is posted as a credit to accounts payable. The rest of the columns are posted as debits. Some of the debits are asset accounts and some are expense accounts. Refer to the illustrated journal and see if you can tell which are assets and which are expenses.

THE ACCOUNTS PAYABLE SUBSIDIARY LEDGER

At about the same time that the clerk is posting totals, he will also post the individual amounts in the amount column as credits to specific accounts payable ledger accounts (Figure 4.9). We have a ledger account for each of our creditors so that we can easily keep track of how much is owed to each of them. These accounts are called *subsidiary ledger accounts,* and the main accounts payable accounts to which we posted the total of our purchase journal is called a *control account.* The sum of the subsidiary accounts will at all times equal the balance of the control account. The subsidiary accounts will not be a part of our trial balance nor will they be on our financial statements. However, they will be balanced with the control account to verify the accuracy of the accounts, and we will often refer to them to determine how much we owe individual creditors.

Subsidiary ledger accounts payable are an important part of our accounting system because much of our accounting activities involve purchases. It is important that we keep an accurate record of how much we owe the individual creditors. Some hotels set up a file for each creditor and do not have separate subsidiary ledger accounts. In small hotels this practice may be acceptable because their volume of transactions is relatively small. However, in larger ones the practice of not keeping subsidiary accounts payable ledgers can be dangerous as it is easy to misplace an invoice.

THE ISSUE JOURNAL

We have set up a system for showing increases in asset and expense accounts through the purchase journal. The food and other inventories will not keep going up in value, but will fall as supplies are used up. When assets are used, they become an expense to the business, and the *issue journal* (Figure 4.10) will record the using of our inventories and the increasing of expenses. It is a relatively simple journal which, when the columns are posted to the general ledger, will credit the inventory and debit the expense (Figure 4.11).

As food is needed from our food inventory, a requisition (Figure 4.12) is prepared and signed by the department head. The storeroom clerk will fill the order in much the same way he would fill an order at the local grocery store. The clerk gathers all the items together and puts the cost of each item on the requisition. The food is given to the department, and the totaled requisition is sent to the accounting depart-

SHEET NO. _____						ACCOUNT NO. 222		
TERMS		NAME	*Allen Meats*					
RATING		ADDRESS						
CREDIT LIMIT								

DATE 19	ITEMS	FOLIO	✓	DEBITS	DATE 19	ITEMS	FOLIO	✓	CREDITS
					June 2				85 75
					4				23 70

FIGURE 4.9.   A LEDGER ACCOUNT FROM THE ACCOUNTS PAYABLE SUBSIDIARY LEDGER.

ment to be entered into the issue journal. Food issued to the kitchen immediately becomes an expense to the hotel.

A WORD ABOUT STOREROOM OPERATION

Food received by the storeroom clerk is checked in and placed on shelves. The clerk will stamp the price of each item on the container so that he can later determine its cost without having to refer to the invoice. He will also date each item so that he can later tell when it was received. As goods stay on the shelf for a period of time, the clerk will refer to the dates to be sure that they are used before they become old and spoil.

He will enter the date and the amount of goods received on the *stock record card* (Figure 4.13). These cards are the clerk's inventory cards. He keeps a record of the quantities of each item received and issued on these cards. Each card will contain the name and address of the supplier as well as the par stock amount. Par stock is that minimal level we let our inventories get to before we reorder. The level is determined by the usage of the item and the amount of time it takes to receive the ordered goods. For example, if we were to use an average of two cases of No. 10 cans of tomatoes each week and it took a week to receive the goods once the order is placed, our par stock might be two cases plus an extra case as a safety precaution, in the event of heavy usage or delay in receiving the goods. Our objective is to have enough food on hand to meet our requirements but not have so much that we run out of storeroom space or tie up too much money in inventory. At the end of the month, the storeroom clerk or one of the stewards will take

Issue Journal

Credit stores

	Date	Requisition number	1 Food	2 Liquor	3 Housekeeping supplies	4
1	1	121	8 73			
2	1	122	25 50			
3	1	202		21 -		
4	1	310			15 -	
5	1	123	34 70			
6	2	124	24 50			
7	2	125	10 30			
8	2	203		33 -		
9	2	311			12 50	
10			103 73	54 -	27 50	
11						
12						
13			Credit inventories			
14						
15						
16						

FIGURE 4.10. ISSUE JOURNAL.

a physical inventory of goods. The actual amount in the storeroom will be compared with the book figure, and we will adjust our book figure to reflect its true value. At any time, the storeroom clerk can compare his stock record card balance with the quantity of a good on the shelf. This procedure helps him keep control over his inventory.

Issues from Other Storerooms

The same procedure is used in other storerooms in the hotel. Requisitions are made out as goods are issued, and the requisitions are sent to the accounting department where they are posted to the issue journal. At the end of the month, physical inventories are taken, and the book inventory figures are adjusted by an adjusting entry so that our books will reflect accurate amounts.

Debit Expense

Food expense	Liquor expense	Housekeeping supply expense	8	9	10	11	12
8 73							
25 50							
		21 -					
		15 -					
34 70							
24 50							
10 30							
	33 -						
		12 50					
103 73	54 -	27 50					

Debit expenses

THE CONTROLS BUILT INTO OUR ACCOUNTING SYSTEM

Our accounting system has certain controls built into it. Let us pause for a moment to explicitly state them.

The sale of food in the dining room is controlled because we verify that all guest checks are accounted for. No item of food is given to a waiter without a written order, the duplicate of the guest check. If we verify that all guest checks are accounted for by number at the end of each meal, it is very difficult for a waiter to give a meal to someone and not charge him for it.

The sale of liquor in the bar and dining room is controlled in the same way as food. However, control of liquor sales is more difficult

SHEET NO. _____   ACCOUNT NO. 121
TERMS   NAME   Food Inventory
RATING   ADDRESS
CREDIT LIMIT

DATE 19		ITEMS	FOLIO	/	DEBITS	DATE 19		ITEMS	FOLIO	/	CREDITS
June	1	Balance			2350	June	30		Id		10373
	30		PJ		5645						

SHEET NO. _____   ACCOUNT NO. 122
TERMS   NAME   Housekeeping Inventory
RATING   ADDRESS
CREDIT LIMIT

DATE 19		ITEMS	FOLIO	/	DEBITS	DATE 19		ITEMS	FOLIO	/	CREDITS
June	30		PJ		70 -	June	30		IJ		2750

SHEET NO. _____   ACCOUNT NO. 123
TERMS   NAME   Liquor Inventory
RATING   ADDRESS
CREDIT LIMIT

DATE 19		ITEMS	FOLIO	/	DEBITS	DATE 19		ITEMS	FOLIO	/	CREDITS
June	1	Balance			890 -	June	30				

SHEET NO. _____   ACCOUNT NO. 510
TERMS   NAME   Food Expense
RATING   ADDRESS
CREDIT LIMIT

DATE 19		ITEMS	FOLIO	/	DEBITS	DATE 19		ITEMS	FOLIO	/	CREDITS
June	30		PJ		47 -						
	30		Id		10373						

SHEET NO. _____   ACCOUNT NO. 521
TERMS   NAME   Liquor Expense
RATING   ADDRESS
CREDIT LIMIT

DATE 19		ITEMS	FOLIO	/	DEBITS	DATE 19		ITEMS	FOLIO	/	CREDITS
June	30		IJ		54 -						

FIGURE 4.11.   LEDGER ACCOUNTS FROM THE ISSUE JOURNAL.

SHEET NO.								ACCOUNT NO. _591_		
TERMS		NAME	*Housekeeping Supply Expense*							
RATING		ADDRESS								
CREDIT LIMIT										

DATE 19	ITEMS	FOLIO	✓	DEBITS	DATE 19	ITEMS	FOLIO	✓	CREDITS
June 30		P.J		8 50					
30		J.J		27 50					

FIGURE 4.11. (Continued.)

than food, because often the same person who mixes the drinks also writes out the order and takes the cash.

The control of all income is verified by the night auditor. All sales must be posted to guest accounts or collected as cash because the night auditor makes certain the total charges and cash sales on his transcript of guest ledger agrees with the total sales of each department.

The control of raw foods is accomplished by rigidly enforcing the ordering, receiving, storing, and issuing routine. The ordering system assures us that we are ordering only those items needed at the lowest possible price and the highest quality consistent with our needs. The receiving routine, when rigidly enforced, assures us that we receive goods exactly as they were ordered. The storage and issuing routine gives us reasonable assurance that goods will remain in good condition until used and that they will not be issued unless authorized by the proper person.

Our accounting system also provides us with a means of checking our progress during the month. We know our daily sales of goods and we know our daily costs. We can compute a food cost or a liquor cost percentage on a daily basis. If our prices reflect a planned cost percentage, we can determine each day how well we are doing. For example, our food cost percentage is determined by

$$\frac{\text{Actual cost of food}}{\text{Sales of food}}$$

If our actual cost of food for a day is $100 and our sales of food for a day are $300, the food cost percentage is 33 percent. We compare that figure with our planned food cost percentage, and we can determine how well we are controlling our costs.

We also know our daily sales for rooms and other departments

REQUISITION ORDER

No. *121*   Date *June 1*   19

To *Food stores*

Please deliver to *Kitchen*

6	#2½ Tomatoe puree		1.88
10	lb. Hamburger	.45	4.50
3	lb. Celery	.20	.60
5	lb. Tomatoes	.35	1.75
			$8.73

Remarks

J. P. Jones **Signature**

Wm. Allen & Co., N. Y. Stock Form 6131   3①3053R   Printed in U.S.A.

FIGURE 4.12.   REQUISITION FROM STORES.

STOCK RECORD CARD

Item   Tomato puree

Supplier   J.C. Smart

            Bridgeport, Conn.

Unit Size   #2½

Price $7.50 case   Par Stock   24

Date	In	Out	Balance
5/31			24
6/1		6	18
6/2		4	14

FIGURE 4.13.   A STOCK RECORD CARD.

within the hotel. We can compare these figures to last week's sales, last month's sales, or last year's sales to determine if things are going well.

SUMMARY

The accounting records for purchases are set up to ensure adequate controls. Food is one of the most often purchased items in a hotel, and the routine for purchasing food must be rigorously followed if adequate control over purchasing is to be maintained. The steward and chef determine the menu, and the steward or purchasing agent orders perishable items on the basis of the menus for the coming period. The steward uses the steward's market quotation list when ordering and circles the price of the items ordered from each purveyor. The accounting department and the receiving clerk each receive a copy of the steward's market quotation list. The receiving clerk will use it to verify receipt of only those items ordered, and the accounting department will use it to verify the correct price for each item.

All received goods will be entered on the receiving clerk's daily report, and that information will be transferred to the purchase journal. Other bills will also be entered in the purchase journal as they are received. At the end of the month, the purchase journal will be added, and the totals will be posted to ledger accounts.

As goods are issued from the storeroom, requisitions will be completed and signed by the department head. The requisitions will be entered in the issue journal. At the end of the month, the issue journal will be added and the totals will be posted to ledger accounts, crediting the appropriate inventory account and debiting the appropriate expense.

The storeroom clerk will maintain a perpetual inventory of all goods under his control. At the end of the month, he will take a physical inventory, and the count will be compared with the book figure. The book figure will be adjusted to reflect the true value of the stock.

QUESTIONS FOR DISCUSSION

1. Which columns in Figure 4.7 are assets and which are expenses?
2. Why are the individual accounts payable ledger accounts called subsidiary accounts?
3. Why are perishable foods ordered over the phone by the steward or purchasing agent and nonperishable items ordered automatically when their par level is reached?
4. Explain the importance of par stock for nonperishable foods.
5. Explain what might happen if steps 1 or 2 in the receiving routine were not followed.
6. If the receiving clerk verified that all invoices were correct, why would he also need to fill in the receiving clerk's daily report?
7. Explain the importance of the invoice stamp to proper control of purchases.
8. Food issued to the kitchen immediately becomes an expense to the hotel. If all of it is not used that day, wouldn't our expenses for the day be overstated? What effect will this have on the food cost over a period of several days?
9. Stock record cards help the storeroom clerk keep a record of all foods

in his storeroom. Explain how they help him keep control over his inventory.

10. Explain why control of liquor can be more difficult than control of food.

11. If food sales for the day are $500 and food cost for the day is $125, compute the food cost percentage. If food sales for the second day are $600 and food cost is $172, compute the overall food cost percentage for the two days.

5 | Accounting for Wages

Wages are the single most important expense to the hotel, accounting for about 40 percent of all expenditures. We will, therefore, treat it as a separate subject and devote a chapter to the computation of pay and the bookkeeping procedures involved.

LEGISLATION AFFECTING WAGES

In recent years the federal government and most state governments have enacted legislation to protect employees from unscrupulous employers and to ensure that everyone working gets paid a minimum wage and extra pay for overtime.

Most states today require that all employees, except management personnel, be paid a minimum rate per hour and overtime pay after five consecutive days or 40 hours of work per week. The department of labor in most states audits the pay records of hotels to verify that they are conforming to the regulations.

COMPUTATION OF PAY

As employees are hired, each must fill in a withholding exemption certificate (form W-4) stating the number of dependents they have (Figure 5.1). Employees may declare fewer dependents than they actually have, but they are not allowed to declare more than they are legally allowed. For example, a man with a wife and two children can

FIGURE 5.1. W-4 EXEMPTION CERTIFICATE FORM.

normally declare four dependents, one for each member of the family. Or he may claim as few as zero. However, he may not declare more than four unless certain members of the family are eligible for additional exemptions due to blindness, old age, or other reasons. The amount of withholding tax taken out of an employee's paycheck is determined by the number of exemptions declared. Fewer exemptions means more withholding tax is deducted. Many employees purposely do not declare their legal number of exemptions, preferring to use the government as a kind of savings account.

Many hotels require each employee to sign a contract card outlining the terms of employment: wage rate, hours of work, restrictions, vacations, etc. This form is a permanent part of the employee's record and is used for the determination of pay as well as an audit of the payroll.

Employees' pay is determined as follows:

Gross wages

+ Tips
_____

= Taxable wages for federal and state withholding tax purposes

+ *Value of room and board*
_____

= Taxable wages for social security tax purposes

Gross wages
— Deductions from pay (withholding taxes, social
security taxes, etc.)

= Net cash wages

Some hotels do not provide free room and board but charge employees for meals and lodging. The computation of pay in such instances is a bit different. It is presented here only to show the difference in computation, since very few hotels charge employees for room and board.

Gross wages
+ *Tips*

= Taxable wages for social security tax purposes
— *Value of room and board*

= Taxable wages for federal and state withholding
tax purposes

Gross wages
— *Value of room and board*

= Cash wages
— *Deductions from pay*

= Net cash wages

The above method results in lesser amounts deducted for social security and withholding taxes. However, it also means a lower paycheck, because the value of room and board is deducted from pay.

Usually, hotels provide employees with meals at no charge when their hours of work overlap a meal hour. Some employees may live in the hotel, and the hotel will usually provide the room free of charge. We will assume that the hotel is providing free room and board in our further discussion, and all illustrations will use the first method of pay computation.

Gross Wages

Gross wages are calculated by adding the normal wage to any overtime that the employee has. The pay for some jobs in the hotel will be based on an hourly wage, and the pay for others may be based on a weekly or monthly wage. Any employee who works for an hourly wage will be required to check in and out and will maintain a time card. The time cards will be used as a basis for determining the number of hours the employee has worked and thus his gross pay. However, simply because the employee has checked into the hotel is no guarantee that he is working. Many hotels require that department supervisors also maintain records of the hours worked by all of their employees. The two records will be compared and any discrepancy will be taken up with the department head. Some states require that time records be maintained for all employees, even though they work on a weekly rate of pay. One purpose of these regulations is to ascertain that employees are being paid overtime for working beyond the state regulated number of days or hours.

Gross pay for a maid—we will call her Joan—working 40 hours a week at $2 per hour plus $3 per hour for overtime would be calculated as shown in Table 5.1. We will assume that overtime starts after eight hours on any given day or more than five days' work per week.

Table 5.1. COMPUTATION OF GROSS PAY

Day	Number of hours worked	Regular pay	Overtime pay	Total gross pay
Monday	8	$16.00	—	$ 16.00
Tuesday	9	16.00	$ 3.00	19.00
Wednesday	10	16.00	6.00	22.00
Thursday	8	16.00	—	16.00
Friday	8	16.00	—	16.00
Saturday	4		12.00	12.00
	47	$80.00	$21.00	$101.00

Tips

All employees who receive tips must declare them. The hotel will issue to each employee a form for declaring such tips and the employee will return it to the accounting department for inclusion in pay records. It is not up to the hotel to determine whether or not the employee is declaring the full amount of tips he actually receives unless the hotel has knowledge that would contradict the employee's declaration. Internal Revenue holds that each employee is responsible for his own honesty. The value of the tips is added to the gross pay to determine taxable pay for withholding tax purposes. That figure is used to determine how much will be deducted from gross pay for withholding tax.

For example, the total gross pay for our maid, Joan, was $101. If she declared $10 in tips for the week, her total taxable salary for withholding tax purposes would be $111.

Value of Room and Board

Technically, room and board is taxable pay and considered a part of the salary. However, if meals are furnished for the employer's convenience and on his premises and lodging is provided as a condition of employment and on the employer's premises, room and board are exempt from the calculation of pay for withholding purposes. The above situation is usually the case in most hotels, so room and board will not be a part of the salary when determining a figure for withholding tax.

However, all room and board must be considered a part of the employee's salary for social security purposes. We will add the value of room and board to salary to arrive at a figure for social security purposes.

Assume that Joan received one meal each day she worked and the value of each meal was 50¢. The total amount of board added to her salary would be $3, bringing her total salary for social security purposes to $114.

Deductions

Certain deductions from pay are required by law. Two of them are withholding tax and social security tax. Tax tables are used to determine how much is deducted for each employee. There are tables for daily, weekly, biweekly (every two weeks), monthly, and semimonthly (every half month) pay periods. Tax tables are also provided for married and single persons because more is usually deducted from the wages of single workers. Most hotels will pay weekly or biweekly. Assume Joan is paid weekly, is married, and claims two exemptions. Her pay for withholding purposes was $111. Referring to the illustrated chart (Figure 5.2), we would deduct $10.70 for withholding tax. Social security tax (Figure 5.3) would be deducted on the basis of a salary of $114, and would be $5.93.

We might also have to deduct other taxes. If we live in a state with a state income tax, the state withholding tax will be deducted from Joan's salary (Figure 5.4). In New York State, the state withholding tax on her salary is $1.70. If our city has a city income tax (as does New York City), a city tax deduction will be made. Other deductions might include union dues, employee's contributions to retirement or health insurance funds, and advances in salary received earlier.

MARRIED Persons — WEEKLY Payroll Period

And the wages are—		And the number of withholding exemptions claimed is—										
At least	But less than	0	1	2	3	4	5	6	7	8	9	10 or more
		The amount of income tax to be withheld shall be—										
$0	$21	$0	$0	$0	$0	$0	$0	$0	$0	$0	$0	$0
21	22	.20	0	0	0	0	0	0	0	0	0	0
22	23	.30	0	0	0	0	0	0	0	0	0	0
23	24	.50	0	0	0	0	0	0	0	0	0	0
24	25	.60	0	0	0	0	0	0	0	0	0	0
25	26	.70	0	0	0	0	0	0	0	0	0	0
26	27	.90	0	0	0	0	0	0	0	0	0	0
27	28	1.00	0	0	0	0	0	0	0	0	0	0
28	29	1.20	0	0	0	0	0	0	0	0	0	0
29	30	1.30	0	0	0	0	0	0	0	0	0	0
30	31	1.40	0	0	0	0	0	0	0	0	0	0
31	32	1.60	0	0	0	0	0	0	0	0	0	0
32	33	1.70	0	0	0	0	0	0	0	0	0	0
33	34	1.90	.10	0	0	0	0	0	0	0	0	0
34	35	2.00	.30	0	0	0	0	0	0	0	0	0
35	36	2.10	.40	0	0	0	0	0	0	0	0	0
36	37	2.30	.50	0	0	0	0	0	0	0	0	0
37	38	2.40	.70	0	0	0	0	0	0	0	0	0
38	39	2.60	.80	0	0	0	0	0	0	0	0	0
39	40	2.70	1.00	0	0	0	0	0	0	0	0	0
40	41	2.80	1.10	0	0	0	0	0	0	0	0	0
41	42	3.00	1.20	0	0	0	0	0	0	0	0	0
42	43	3.10	1.40	0	0	0	0	0	0	0	0	0
43	44	3.30	1.50	0	0	0	0	0	0	0	0	0
44	45	3.50	1.70	0	0	0	0	0	0	0	0	0
45	46	3.60	1.80	0	0	0	0	0	0	0	0	0
46	47	3.80	1.90	.20	0	0	0	0	0	0	0	0
47	48	4.00	2.10	.30	0	0	0	0	0	0	0	0
48	49	4.10	2.20	.50	0	0	0	0	0	0	0	0
49	50	4.30	2.40	.60	0	0	0	0	0	0	0	0
50	51	4.50	2.50	.70	0	0	0	0	0	0	0	0
51	52	4.70	2.60	.90	0	0	0	0	0	0	0	0
52	53	4.80	2.80	1.00	0	0	0	0	0	0	0	0
53	54	5.00	2.90	1.20	0	0	0	0	0	0	0	0
54	55	5.20	3.10	1.30	0	0	0	0	0	0	0	0
55	56	5.30	3.20	1.40	0	0	0	0	0	0	0	0
56	57	5.50	3.40	1.60	0	0	0	0	0	0	0	0
57	58	5.70	3.60	1.70	0	0	0	0	0	0	0	0
58	59	5.80	3.70	1.90	.10	0	0	0	0	0	0	0
59	60	6.00	3.90	2.00	.30	0	0	0	0	0	0	0
60	62	6.30	4.10	2.20	.50	0	0	0	0	0	0	0
62	64	6.60	4.50	2.50	.70	0	0	0	0	0	0	0
64	66	7.00	4.80	2.80	1.00	0	0	0	0	0	0	0
66	68	7.30	5.20	3.10	1.30	0	0	0	0	0	0	0
68	70	7.60	5.50	3.40	1.60	0	0	0	0	0	0	0
70	72	8.00	5.80	3.70	1.90	.10	0	0	0	0	0	0
72	74	8.30	6.20	4.10	2.10	.40	0	0	0	0	0	0
74	76	8.70	6.50	4.40	2.40	.70	0	0	0	0	0	0
76	78	9.00	6.90	4.70	2.70	1.00	0	0	0	0	0	0
78	80	9.30	7.20	5.10	3.00	1.20	0	0	0	0	0	0
80	82	9.60	7.50	5.40	3.30	1.50	0	0	0	0	0	0
82	84	10.00	7.90	5.80	3.60	1.80	0	0	0	0	0	0
84	86	10.30	8.20	6.10	4.00	2.10	.30	0	0	0	0	0
86	88	10.60	8.60	6.40	4.30	2.40	.60	0	0	0	0	0
88	90	10.90	8.90	6.80	4.70	2.60	.90	0	0	0	0	0
90	92	11.20	9.20	7.10	5.00	2.90	1.20	0	0	0	0	0
92	94	11.60	9.60	7.50	5.30	3.20	1.40	0	0	0	0	0
94	96	11.90	9.90	7.80	5.70	3.60	1.70	0	0	0	0	0
96	98	12.20	10.20	8.10	6.00	3.90	2.00	.30	0	0	0	0
98	100	12.50	10.50	8.50	6.40	4.20	2.30	.50	0	0	0	0

(Continued on next page)

FIGURE 5.2.   TAX TABLES FOR WITHHOLDING TAX.

MARRIED Persons — WEEKLY Payroll Period

And the wages are—		And the number of withholding exemptions claimed is—										
At least	But less than	0	1	2	3	4	5	6	7	8	9	10 or more
		The amount of income tax to be withheld shall be—										
$100	$105	$13.10	$11.10	$9.10	$7.00	$4.80	$2.80	$1.00	$0	$0	$0	$0
105	110	13.90	11.90	9.90	7.80	5.70	3.60	1.70	0	0	0	0
110	115	14.70	12.70	10.70	8.70	6.50	4.40	2.40	.70	0	0	0
115	120	15.50	13.50	11.50	9.50	7.40	5.30	3.10	1.40	0	0	0
120	125	16.30	14.30	12.30	10.30	8.20	6.10	4.00	2.10	.30	0	0
125	130	17.10	15.10	13.10	11.10	9.10	7.00	4.80	2.80	1.00	0	0
130	135	17.90	15.90	13.90	11.90	9.90	7.80	5.70	3.60	1.70	0	0
135	140	18.70	16.70	14.70	12.70	10.70	8.70	6.50	4.40	2.40	.70	0
140	145	19.50	17.50	15.50	13.50	11.50	9.50	7.40	5.30	3.10	1.40	0
145	150	20.30	18.30	16.30	14.30	12.30	10.30	8.20	6.10	4.00	2.10	.30
150	160	21.50	19.50	17.50	15.50	13.50	11.50	9.50	7.40	5.30	3.10	1.40
160	170	23.10	21.10	19.10	17.10	15.10	13.10	11.10	9.10	7.00	4.80	2.80
170	180	25.00	22.70	20.70	18.70	16.70	14.70	12.70	10.70	8.70	6.50	4.40
180	190	26.90	24.50	22.30	20.30	18.30	16.30	14.30	12.30	10.30	8.20	6.10
190	200	28.80	26.40	24.10	21.90	19.90	17.90	15.90	13.90	11.90	9.90	7.80
200	210	30.70	28.30	26.00	23.60	21.50	19.50	17.50	15.50	13.50	11.50	9.50
210	220	32.60	30.20	27.90	25.50	23.10	21.10	19.10	17.10	15.10	13.10	11.10
220	230	34.50	32.10	29.80	27.40	25.00	22.70	20.70	18.70	16.70	14.70	12.70
230	240	36.40	34.00	31.70	29.30	26.90	24.50	22.30	20.30	18.30	16.30	14.30
240	250	38.30	35.90	33.60	31.20	28.80	26.40	24.10	21.90	19.90	17.90	15.90
250	260	40.20	37.80	35.50	33.10	30.70	28.30	26.00	23.60	21.50	19.50	17.50
260	270	42.10	39.70	37.40	35.00	32.60	30.20	27.90	25.50	23.10	21.10	19.10
270	280	44.10	41.60	39.30	36.90	34.50	32.10	29.80	27.40	25.00	22.70	20.70
280	290	46.20	43.60	41.20	38.80	36.40	34.00	31.70	29.30	26.90	24.50	22.30
290	300	48.30	45.70	43.10	40.70	38.30	35.90	33.60	31.20	28.80	26.40	24.10
300	310	50.40	47.80	45.20	42.60	40.20	37.80	35.50	33.10	30.70	28.30	26.00
310	320	52.50	49.90	47.30	44.70	42.10	39.70	37.40	35.00	32.60	30.20	27.90
320	330	54.60	52.00	49.40	46.80	44.10	41.60	39.30	36.90	34.50	32.10	29.80
330	340	56.70	54.10	51.50	48.90	46.20	43.60	41.20	38.80	36.40	34.00	31.70
340	350	58.80	56.20	53.60	51.00	48.30	45.70	43.10	40.70	38.30	35.90	33.60
350	360	60.90	58.30	55.70	53.10	50.40	47.80	45.20	42.60	40.20	37.80	35.50
360	370	63.00	60.40	57.80	55.20	52.50	49.90	47.30	44.70	42.10	39.70	37.40
370	380	65.10	62.50	59.90	57.30	54.60	52.00	49.40	46.80	44.10	41.60	39.30
380	390	67.30	64.60	62.00	59.40	56.70	54.10	51.50	48.90	46.20	43.60	41.20
390	400	69.80	66.70	64.10	61.50	58.80	56.20	53.60	51.00	48.30	45.70	43.10
400	410	72.30	69.10	66.20	63.60	60.90	58.30	55.70	53.10	50.40	47.80	45.20
410	420	74.80	71.60	68.50	65.70	63.00	60.40	57.80	55.20	52.50	49.90	47.30
420	430	77.30	74.10	71.00	67.90	65.10	62.50	59.90	57.30	54.60	52.00	49.40
430	440	79.80	76.60	73.50	70.40	67.30	64.60	62.00	59.40	56.70	54.10	51.50
440	450	82.30	79.10	76.00	72.90	69.80	66.70	64.10	61.50	58.80	56.20	53.60
450	460	84.80	81.60	78.50	75.40	72.30	69.10	66.20	63.60	60.90	58.30	55.70
460	470	87.30	84.10	81.00	77.90	74.80	71.60	68.50	65.70	63.00	60.40	57.80
470	480	89.80	86.60	83.50	80.40	77.30	74.10	71.00	67.90	65.10	62.50	59.90
480	490	92.30	89.10	86.00	82.90	79.80	76.60	73.50	70.40	67.30	64.60	62.00
490	500	94.80	91.60	88.50	85.40	82.30	79.10	76.00	72.90	69.80	66.70	64.10
500	510	97.30	94.10	91.00	87.90	84.80	81.60	78.50	75.40	72.30	69.10	66.20
510	520	99.80	96.60	93.50	90.40	87.30	84.10	81.00	77.90	74.80	71.60	68.50
520	530	102.30	99.10	96.00	92.90	89.80	86.60	83.50	80.40	77.30	74.10	71.00
		25 percent of the excess over $530 plus—										
$530 and over		103.50	100.40	97.30	94.10	91.00	87.90	84.80	81.60	78.50	75.40	72.30

Social Security Employee Tax Table

5.2 percent employee tax deductions

Wages At least	Wages But less than	Tax to be withheld	Wages At least	Wages But less than	Tax to be withheld	Wages At least	Wages But less than	Tax to be withheld	Wages At least	Wages But less than	Tax to be withheld
$0.00	$0.10	$0.00	$12.41	$12.60	$.65	$24.91	$25.10	$1.30	$37.41	$37.60	$1.95
.10	.29	.01	12.60	12.79	.66	25.10	25.29	1.31	37.60	37.79	1.96
.29	.49	.02	12.79	12.99	.67	25.29	25.49	1.32	37.79	37.99	1.97
.49	.68	.03	12.99	13.18	.68	25.49	25.68	1.33	37.99	38.18	1.98
.68	.87	.04	13.18	13.37	.69	25.68	25.87	1.34	38.18	38.37	1.99
.87	1.06	.05	13.37	13.56	.70	25.87	26.06	1.35	38.37	38.56	2.00
1.06	1.25	.06	13.56	13.75	.71	26.06	26.25	1.36	38.56	38.75	2.01
1.25	1.45	.07	13.75	13.95	.72	26.25	26.45	1.37	38.75	38.95	2.02
1.45	1.64	.08	13.95	14.14	.73	26.45	26.64	1.38	38.95	39.14	2.03
1.64	1.83	.09	14.14	14.33	.74	26.64	26.83	1.39	39.14	39.33	2.04
1.83	2.02	.10	14.33	14.52	.75	26.83	27.02	1.40	39.33	39.52	2.05
2.02	2.22	.11	14.52	14.72	.76	27.02	27.22	1.41	39.52	39.72	2.06
2.22	2.41	.12	14.72	14.91	.77	27.22	27.41	1.42	39.72	39.91	2.07
2.41	2.60	.13	14.91	15.10	.78	27.41	27.60	1.43	39.91	40.10	2.08
2.60	2.79	.14	15.10	15.29	.79	27.60	27.79	1.44	40.10	40.29	2.09
2.79	2.99	.15	15.29	15.49	.80	27.79	27.99	1.45	40.29	40.49	2.10
2.99	3.18	.16	15.49	15.68	.81	27.99	28.18	1.46	40.49	40.68	2.11
3.18	3.37	.17	15.68	15.87	.82	28.18	28.37	1.47	40.68	40.87	2.12
3.37	3.56	.18	15.87	16.06	.83	28.37	28.56	1.48	40.87	41.06	2.13
3.56	3.75	.19	16.06	16.25	.84	28.56	28.75	1.49	41.06	41.25	2.14
3.75	3.95	.20	16.25	16.45	.85	28.75	28.95	1.50	41.25	41.45	2.15
3.95	4.14	.21	16.45	16.64	.86	28.95	29.14	1.51	41.45	41.64	2.16
4.14	4.33	.22	16.64	16.83	.87	29.14	29.33	1.52	41.64	41.83	2.17
4.33	4.52	.23	16.83	17.02	.88	29.33	29.52	1.53	41.83	42.02	2.18
4.52	4.72	.24	17.02	17.22	.89	29.52	29.72	1.54	42.02	42.22	2.19
4.72	4.91	.25	17.22	17.41	.90	29.72	29.91	1.55	42.22	42.41	2.20
4.91	5.10	.26	17.41	17.60	.91	29.91	30.10	1.56	42.41	42.60	2.21
5.10	5.29	.27	17.60	17.79	.92	30.10	30.29	1.57	42.60	42.79	2.22
5.29	5.49	.28	17.79	17.99	.93	30.29	30.49	1.58	42.79	42.99	2.23
5.49	5.68	.29	17.99	18.18	.94	30.49	30.68	1.59	42.99	43.18	2.24
5.68	5.87	.30	18.18	18.37	.95	30.68	30.87	1.60	43.18	43.37	2.25
5.87	6.06	.31	18.37	18.56	.96	30.87	31.06	1.61	43.37	43.56	2.26
6.06	6.25	.32	18.56	18.75	.97	31.06	31.25	1.62	43.56	43.75	2.27
6.25	6.45	.33	18.75	18.95	.98	31.25	31.45	1.63	43.75	43.95	2.28
6.45	6.64	.34	18.95	19.14	.99	31.45	31.64	1.64	43.95	44.14	2.29
6.64	6.83	.35	19.14	19.33	1.00	31.64	31.83	1.65	44.14	44.33	2.30
6.83	7.02	.36	19.33	19.52	1.01	31.83	32.02	1.66	44.33	44.52	2.31
7.02	7.22	.37	19.52	19.72	1.02	32.02	32.22	1.67	44.52	44.72	2.32
7.22	7.41	.38	19.72	19.91	1.03	32.22	32.41	1.68	44.72	44.91	2.33
7.41	7.60	.39	19.91	20.10	1.04	32.41	32.60	1.69	44.91	45.10	2.34
7.60	7.79	.40	20.10	20.29	1.05	32.60	32.79	1.70	45.10	45.29	2.35
7.79	7.99	.41	20.29	20.49	1.06	32.79	32.99	1.71	45.29	45.49	2.36
7.99	8.18	.42	20.49	20.68	1.07	32.99	33.18	1.72	45.49	45.68	2.37
8.18	8.37	.43	20.68	20.87	1.08	33.18	33.37	1.73	45.68	45.87	2.38
8.37	8.56	.44	20.87	21.06	1.09	33.37	33.56	1.74	45.87	46.06	2.39
8.56	8.75	.45	21.06	21.25	1.10	33.56	33.75	1.75	46.06	46.25	2.40
8.75	8.95	.46	21.25	21.45	1.11	33.75	33.95	1.76	46.25	46.45	2.41
8.95	9.14	.47	21.45	21.64	1.12	33.95	34.14	1.77	46.45	46.64	2.42
9.14	9.33	.48	21.64	21.83	1.13	34.14	34.33	1.78	46.64	46.83	2.43
9.33	9.52	.49	21.83	22.02	1.14	34.33	34.52	1.79	46.83	47.02	2.44
9.52	9.72	.50	22.02	22.22	1.15	34.52	34.72	1.80	47.02	47.22	2.45
9.72	9.91	.51	22.22	22.41	1.16	34.72	34.91	1.81	47.22	47.41	2.46
9.91	10.10	.52	22.41	22.60	1.17	34.91	35.10	1.82	47.41	47.60	2.47
10.10	10.29	.53	22.60	22.79	1.18	35.10	35.29	1.83	47.60	47.79	2.48
10.29	10.49	.54	22.79	22.99	1.19	35.29	35.49	1.84	47.79	47.99	2.49
10.49	10.68	.55	22.99	23.18	1.20	35.49	35.68	1.85	47.99	48.18	2.50
10.68	10.87	.56	23.18	23.37	1.21	35.68	35.87	1.86	48.18	48.37	2.51
10.87	11.06	.57	23.37	23.56	1.22	35.87	36.06	1.87	48.37	48.56	2.52
11.06	11.25	.58	23.56	23.75	1.23	36.06	36.25	1.88	48.56	48.75	2.53
11.25	11.45	.59	23.75	23.95	1.24	36.25	36.45	1.89	48.75	48.95	2.54
11.45	11.64	.60	23.95	24.14	1.25	36.45	36.64	1.90	48.95	49.14	2.55
11.64	11.83	.61	24.14	24.33	1.26	36.64	36.83	1.91	49.14	49.33	2.56
11.83	12.02	.62	24.33	24.52	1.27	36.83	37.02	1.92	49.33	49.52	2.57
12.02	12.22	.63	24.52	24.72	1.28	37.02	37.22	1.93	49.52	49.72	2.58
12.22	12.41	.64	24.72	24.91	1.29	37.22	37.41	1.94	49.72	49.91	2.59

FIGURE 5.3. TAX TABLES FOR SOCIAL SECURITY.

Social Security Employee Tax Table—Continued

5.2 percent employee tax deductions

Wages		Tax to be withheld	Wages		Tax to be withheld	Wages		Tax to be withheld	Wages		Tax to be withheld
At least	But less than		At least	But less than		At least	But less than		At least	But less than	
$49.91	$50.10	$2.60	$62.41	$62.60	$3.25	$74.91	$75.10	$3.90	$87.41	$87.60	$4.55
50.10	50.29	2.61	62.60	62.79	3.26	75.10	75.29	3.91	87.60	87.79	4.56
50.29	50.49	2.62	62.79	62.99	3.27	75.29	75.49	3.92	87.79	87.99	4.57
50.49	50.68	2.63	62.99	63.18	3.28	75.49	75.68	3.93	87.99	88.18	4.58
50.68	50.87	2.64	63.18	63.37	3.29	75.68	75.87	3.94	88.18	88.37	4.59
50.87	51.06	2.65	63.37	63.56	3.30	75.87	76.06	3.95	88.37	88.56	4.60
51.06	51.25	2.66	63.56	63.75	3.31	76.06	76.25	3.96	88.56	88.75	4.61
51.25	51.45	2.67	63.75	63.95	3.32	76.25	76.45	3.97	88.75	88.95	4.62
51.45	51.64	2.68	63.95	64.14	3.33	76.45	76.64	3.98	88.95	89.14	4.63
51.64	51.83	2.69	64.14	64.33	3.34	76.64	76.83	3.99	89.14	89.33	4.64
51.83	52.02	2.70	64.33	64.52	3.35	76.83	77.02	4.00	89.33	89.52	4.65
52.02	52.22	2.71	64.52	64.72	3.36	77.02	77.22	4.01	89.52	89.72	4.66
52.22	52.41	2.72	64.72	64.91	3.37	77.22	77.41	4.02	89.72	89.91	4.67
52.41	52.60	2.73	64.91	65.10	3.38	77.41	77.60	4.03	89.91	90.10	4.68
52.60	52.79	2.74	65.10	65.29	3.39	77.60	77.79	4.04	90.10	90.29	4.69
52.79	52.99	2.75	65.29	65.49	3.40	77.79	77.99	4.05	90.29	90.49	4.70
52.99	53.18	2.76	65.49	65.68	3.41	77.99	78.18	4.06	90.49	90.68	4.71
53.18	53.37	2.77	65.68	65.87	3.42	78.18	78.37	4.07	90.68	90.87	4.72
53.37	53.56	2.78	65.87	66.06	3.43	78.37	78.56	4.08	90.87	91.06	4.73
53.56	53.75	2.79	66.06	66.25	3.44	78.56	78.75	4.09	91.06	91.25	4.74
53.75	53.95	2.80	66.25	66.45	3.45	78.75	78.95	4.10	91.25	91.45	4.75
53.95	54.14	2.81	66.45	66.64	3.46	78.95	79.14	4.11	91.45	91.64	4.76
54.14	54.33	2.82	66.64	66.83	3.47	79.14	79.33	4.12	91.64	91.83	4.77
54.33	54.52	2.83	66.83	67.02	3.48	79.33	79.52	4.13	91.83	92.02	4.78
54.52	54.72	2.84	67.02	67.22	3.49	79.52	79.72	4.14	92.02	92.22	4.79
54.72	54.91	2.85	67.22	67.41	3.50	79.72	79.91	4.15	92.22	92.41	4.80
54.91	55.10	2.86	67.41	67.60	3.51	79.91	80.10	4.16	92.41	92.60	4.81
55.10	55.29	2.87	67.60	67.79	3.52	80.10	80.29	4.17	92.60	92.79	4.82
55.29	55.49	2.88	67.79	67.99	3.53	80.29	80.49	4.18	92.79	92.99	4.83
55.49	55.68	2.89	67.99	68.18	3.54	80.49	80.68	4.19	92.99	93.18	4.84
55.68	55.87	2.90	68.18	68.37	3.55	80.68	80.87	4.20	93.18	93.37	4.85
55.87	56.06	2.91	68.37	68.56	3.56	80.87	81.06	4.21	93.37	93.56	4.86
56.06	56.25	2.92	68.56	68.75	3.57	81.06	81.25	4.22	93.56	93.75	4.87
56.25	56.45	2.93	68.75	68.95	3.58	81.25	81.45	4.23	93.75	93.95	4.88
56.45	56.64	2.94	68.95	69.14	3.59	81.45	81.64	4.24	93.95	94.14	4.89
56.64	56.83	2.95	69.14	69.33	3.60	81.64	81.83	4.25	94.14	94.33	4.90
56.83	57.02	2.96	69.33	69.52	3.61	81.83	82.02	4.26	94.33	94.52	4.91
57.02	57.22	2.97	69.52	69.72	3.62	82.02	82.22	4.27	94.52	94.72	4.92
57.22	57.41	2.98	69.72	69.91	3.63	82.22	82.41	4.28	94.72	94.91	4.93
57.41	57.60	2.99	69.91	70.10	3.64	82.41	82.60	4.29	94.91	95.10	4.94
57.60	57.79	3.00	70.10	70.29	3.65	82.60	82.79	4.30	95.10	95.29	4.95
57.79	57.99	3.01	70.29	70.49	3.66	82.79	82.99	4.31	95.29	95.49	4.96
57.99	58.18	3.02	70.49	70.68	3.67	82.99	83.18	4.32	95.49	95.68	4.97
58.18	58.37	3.03	70.68	70.87	3.68	83.18	83.37	4.33	95.68	95.87	4.98
58.37	58.56	3.04	70.87	71.06	3.69	83.37	83.56	4.34	95.87	96.06	4.99
58.56	58.75	3.05	71.06	71.25	3.70	83.56	83.75	4.35	96.06	96.25	5.00
58.75	58.95	3.06	71.25	71.45	3.71	83.75	83.95	4.36	96.25	96.45	5.01
58.95	59.14	3.07	71.45	71.64	3.72	83.95	84.14	4.37	96.45	96.64	5.02
59.14	59.33	3.08	71.64	71.83	3.73	84.14	84.33	4.38	96.64	96.83	5.03
59.33	59.52	3.09	71.83	72.02	3.74	84.33	84.52	4.39	96.83	97.02	5.04
59.52	59.72	3.10	72.02	72.22	3.75	84.52	84.72	4.40	97.02	97.22	5.05
59.72	59.91	3.11	72.22	72.41	3.76	84.72	84.91	4.41	97.22	97.41	5.06
59.91	60.10	3.12	72.41	72.60	3.77	84.91	85.10	4.42	97.41	97.60	5.07
60.10	60.29	3.13	72.60	72.79	3.78	85.10	85.29	4.43	97.60	97.79	5.08
60.29	60.49	3.14	72.79	72.99	3.79	85.29	85.49	4.44	97.79	97.99	5.09
60.49	60.68	3.15	72.99	73.18	3.80	85.49	85.68	4.45	97.99	98.18	5.10
60.68	60.87	3.16	73.18	73.37	3.81	85.68	85.87	4.46	98.18	98.37	5.11
60.87	61.06	3.17	73.37	73.56	3.82	85.87	86.06	4.47	98.37	98.56	5.12
61.06	61.25	3.18	73.56	73.75	3.83	86.06	86.25	4.48	98.56	98.75	5.13
61.25	61.45	3.19	73.75	73.95	3.84	86.25	86.45	4.49	98.75	98.95	5.14
61.45	61.64	3.20	73.95	74.14	3.85	86.45	86.64	4.50	98.95	99.14	5.15
61.64	61.83	3.21	74.14	74.33	3.86	86.64	86.83	4.51	99.14	99.33	5.16
61.83	62.02	3.22	74.33	74.52	3.87	86.83	87.02	4.52	99.33	99.52	5.17
62.02	62.22	3.23	74.52	74.72	3.88	87.02	87.22	4.53	99.52	99.72	5.18
62.22	62.41	3.24	74.72	74.91	3.89	87.22	87.41	4.54	99.72	99.91	5.19

Social Security Employee Tax Table—Continued

5.2 percent employee tax deductions

Wages At least	Wages But less than	Tax to be withheld	Wages At least	Wages But less than	Tax to be withheld	Wages At least	Wages But less than	Tax to be withheld	Wages At least	Wages But less than	Tax to be withheld
$99.91	$100.10	$5.20	$112.41	$112.60	$5.85	$124.91	$125.10	$6.50	$137.41	$137.60	$7.15
100.10	100.29	5.21	112.60	112.79	5.86	125.10	125.29	6.51	137.60	137.79	7.16
100.29	100.49	5.22	112.79	112.99	5.87	125.29	125.49	6.52	137.79	137.99	7.17
100.49	100.68	5.23	112.99	113.18	5.88	125.49	125.68	6.53	137.99	138.18	7.18
100.68	100.87	5.24	113.18	113.37	5.89	125.68	125.87	6.54	138.18	138.37	7.19
100.87	101.06	5.25	113.37	113.56	5.90	125.87	126.06	6.55	138.37	138.56	7.20
101.06	101.25	5.26	113.56	113.75	5.91	126.06	126.25	6.56	138.56	138.75	7.21
101.25	101.45	5.27	113.75	113.95	5.92	126.25	126.45	6.57	138.75	138.95	7.22
101.45	101.64	5.28	113.95	114.14	5.93	126.45	126.64	6.58	138.95	139.14	7.23
101.64	101.83	5.29	114.14	114.33	5.94	126.64	126.83	6.59	139.14	139.33	7.24
101.83	102.02	5.30	114.33	114.52	5.95	126.83	127.02	6.60	139.33	139.52	7.25
102.02	102.22	5.31	114.52	114.72	5.96	127.02	127.22	6.61	139.52	139.72	7.26
102.22	102.41	5.32	114.72	114.91	5.97	127.22	127.41	6.62	139.72	139.91	7.27
102.41	102.60	5.33	114.91	115.10	5.98	127.41	127.60	6.63	139.91	140.10	7.28
102.60	102.79	5.34	115.10	115.29	5.99	127.60	127.79	6.64	140.10	140.29	7.29
102.79	102.99	5.35	115.29	115.49	6.00	127.79	127.99	6.65	140.29	140.49	7.30
102.99	103.18	5.36	115.49	115.68	6.01	127.99	128.18	6.66	140.49	140.68	7.31
103.18	103.37	5.37	115.68	115.87	6.02	128.18	128.37	6.67	140.68	140.87	7.32
103.37	103.56	5.38	115.87	116.06	6.03	128.37	128.56	6.68	140.87	141.06	7.33
103.56	103.75	5.39	116.06	116.25	6.04	128.56	128.75	6.69	141.06	141.25	7.34
103.75	103.95	5.40	116.25	116.45	6.05	128.75	128.95	6.70	141.25	141.45	7.35
103.95	104.14	5.41	116.45	116.64	6.06	128.95	129.14	6.71	141.45	141.64	7.36
104.14	104.33	5.42	116.64	116.83	6.07	129.14	129.33	6.72	141.64	141.83	7.37
104.33	104.52	5.43	116.83	117.02	6.08	129.33	129.52	6.73	141.83	142.02	7.38
104.52	104.72	5.44	117.02	117.22	6.09	129.52	129.72	6.74	142.02	142.22	7.39
104.72	104.91	5.45	117.22	117.41	6.10	129.72	129.91	6.75	142.22	142.41	7.40
104.91	105.10	5.46	117.41	117.60	6.11	129.91	130.10	6.76	142.41	142.60	7.41
105.10	105.29	5.47	117.60	117.79	6.12	130.10	130.29	6.77	142.60	142.79	7.42
105.29	105.49	5.48	117.79	117.99	6.13	130.29	130.49	6.78	142.79	142.99	7.43
105.49	105.68	5.49	117.99	118.18	6.14	130.49	130.68	6.79	142.99	143.18	7.44
105.68	105.87	5.50	118.18	118.37	6.15	130.68	130.87	6.80	143.18	143.37	7.45
105.87	106.06	5.51	118.37	118.56	6.16	130.87	131.06	6.81	143.37	143.56	7.46
106.06	106.25	5.52	118.56	118.75	6.17	131.06	131.25	6.82	143.56	143.75	7.47
106.25	106.45	5.53	118.75	118.95	6.18	131.25	131.45	6.83	143.75	143.95	7.48
106.45	106.64	5.54	118.95	119.14	6.19	131.45	131.64	6.84	143.95	144.14	7.49
106.64	106.83	5.55	119.14	119.33	6.20	131.64	131.83	6.85	144.14	144.33	7.50
106.83	107.02	5.56	119.33	119.52	6.21	131.83	132.02	6.86	144.33	144.52	7.51
107.02	107.22	5.57	119.52	119.72	6.22	132.02	132.22	6.87	144.52	144.72	7.52
107.22	107.41	5.58	119.72	119.91	6.23	132.22	132.41	6.88	144.72	144.91	7.53
107.41	107.60	5.59	119.91	120.10	6.24	132.41	132.60	6.89	144.91	145.10	7.54
107.60	107.79	5.60	120.10	120.29	6.25	132.60	132.79	6.90	145.10	145.29	7.55
107.79	107.99	5.61	120.29	120.49	6.26	132.79	132.99	6.91	145.29	145.49	7.56
107.99	108.18	5.62	120.49	120.68	6.27	132.99	133.18	6.92	145.49	145.68	7.57
108.18	108.37	5.63	120.68	120.87	6.28	133.18	133.37	6.93	145.68	145.87	7.58
108.37	108.56	5.64	120.87	121.06	6.29	133.37	133.56	6.94	145.87	146.06	7.59
108.56	108.75	5.65	121.06	121.25	6.30	133.56	133.75	6.95	146.06	146.25	7.60
108.75	108.95	5.66	121.25	121.45	6.31	133.75	133.95	6.96	146.25	146.45	7.61
108.95	109.14	5.67	121.45	121.64	6.32	133.95	134.14	6.97	146.45	146.64	7.62
109.14	109.33	5.68	121.64	121.83	6.33	134.14	134.33	6.98	146.64	146.83	7.63
109.33	109.52	5.69	121.83	122.02	6.34	134.33	134.52	6.99	146.83	147.02	7.64
109.52	109.72	5.70	122.02	122.22	6.35	134.52	134.72	7.00	147.02	147.22	7.65
109.72	109.91	5.71	122.22	122.41	6.36	134.72	134.91	7.01	147.22	147.41	7.66
109.91	110.10	5.72	122.41	122.60	6.37	134.91	135.10	7.02	147.41	147.60	7.67
110.10	110.29	5.73	122.60	122.79	6.38	135.10	135.29	7.03	147.60	147.79	7.68
110.29	110.49	5.74	122.79	122.99	6.39	135.29	135.49	7.04	147.79	147.99	7.69
110.49	110.68	5.75	122.99	123.18	6.40	135.49	135.68	7.05	147.99	148.18	7.70
110.68	110.87	5.76	123.18	123.37	6.41	135.68	135.87	7.06	148.18	148.37	7.71
110.87	111.06	5.77	123.37	123.56	6.42	135.87	136.06	7.07	148.37	148.56	7.72
111.06	111.25	5.78	123.56	123.75	6.43	136.06	136.25	7.08	148.56	148.75	7.73
111.25	111.45	5.79	123.75	123.95	6.44	136.25	136.45	7.09	148.75	148.95	7.74
111.45	111.64	5.80	123.95	124.14	6.45	136.45	136.64	7.10	148.95	149.14	7.75
111.64	111.83	5.81	124.14	124.33	6.46	136.64	136.83	7.11	149.14	149.33	7.76
111.83	112.02	5.82	124.33	124.52	6.47	136.83	137.02	7.12	149.33	149.52	7.77
112.02	112.22	5.83	124.52	124.72	6.48	137.02	137.22	7.13	149.52	149.72	7.78
112.22	112.41	5.84	124.72	124.91	6.49	137.22	137.41	7.14	149.72	149.91	7.79

FIGURE 5.3. (Continued.)

Social Security Employee Tax Table—Continued

5.2 percent employee tax deductions

Wages		Tax to be withheld	Wages		Tax to be withheld	Wages		Tax to be withheld	Wages		Tax to be withheld
At least	But less than		At least	But less than		At least	But less than		At least	But less than	
$149.91	$150.10	$7.80	$162.41	$162.60	$8.45	$174.91	$175.10	$9.10	$187.41	$187.60	$9.75
150.10	150.29	7.81	162.60	162.79	8.46	175.10	175.29	9.11	187.60	187.79	9.76
150.29	150.49	7.82	162.79	162.99	8.47	175.29	175.49	9.12	187.79	187.99	9.77
150.49	150.68	7.83	162.99	163.18	8.48	175.49	175.68	9.13	187.99	188.18	9.78
150.68	150.87	7.84	163.18	163.37	8.49	175.68	175.87	9.14	188.18	188.37	9.79
150.87	151.06	7.85	163.37	163.56	8.50	175.87	176.06	9.15	188.37	188.56	9.80
151.06	151.25	7.86	163.56	163.75	8.51	176.06	176.25	9.16	188.56	188.75	9.81
151.25	151.45	7.87	163.75	163.95	8.52	176.25	176.45	9.17	188.75	188.95	9.82
151.45	151.64	7.88	163.95	164.14	8.53	176.45	176.64	9.18	188.95	189.14	9.83
151.64	151.83	7.89	164.14	164.33	8.54	176.64	176.83	9.19	189.14	189.33	9.84
151.83	152.02	7.90	164.33	164.52	8.55	176.83	177.02	9.20	189.33	189.52	9.85
152.02	152.22	7.91	164.52	164.72	8.56	177.02	177.22	9.21	189.52	189.72	9.86
152.22	152.41	7.92	164.72	164.91	8.57	177.22	177.41	9.22	189.72	189.91	9.87
152.41	152.60	7.93	164.91	165.10	8.58	177.41	177.60	9.23	189.91	190.10	9.88
152.60	152.79	7.94	165.10	165.29	8.59	177.60	177.79	9.24	190.10	190.29	9.89
152.79	152.99	7.95	165.29	165.49	8.60	177.79	177.99	9.25	190.29	190.49	9.90
152.99	153.18	7.96	165.49	165.68	8.61	177.99	178.18	9.26	190.49	190.68	9.91
153.18	153.37	7.97	165.68	165.87	8.62	178.18	178.37	9.27	190.68	190.87	9.92
153.37	153.56	7.98	165.87	166.06	8.63	178.37	178.56	9.28	190.87	191.06	9.93
153.56	153.75	7.99	166.06	166.25	8.64	178.56	178.75	9.29	191.06	191.25	9.94
153.75	153.95	8.00	166.25	166.45	8.65	178.75	178.95	9.30	191.25	191.45	9.95
153.95	154.14	8.01	166.45	166.64	8.66	178.95	179.14	9.31	191.45	191.64	9.96
154.14	154.33	8.02	166.64	166.83	8.67	179.14	179.33	9.32	191.64	191.83	9.97
154.33	154.52	8.03	166.83	167.02	8.68	179.33	179.52	9.33	191.83	192.02	9.98
154.52	154.72	8.04	167.02	167.22	8.69	179.52	179.72	9.34	192.02	192.22	9.99
154.72	154.91	8.05	167.22	167.41	8.70	179.72	179.91	9.35	192.22	192.41	10.00
154.91	155.10	8.06	167.41	167.60	8.71	179.91	180.10	9.36	192.41	192.60	10.01
155.10	155.29	8.07	167.60	167.79	8.72	180.10	180.29	9.37	192.60	192.79	10.02
155.29	155.49	8.08	167.79	167.99	8.73	180.29	180.49	9.38	192.79	192.99	10.03
155.49	155.68	8.09	167.99	168.18	8.74	180.49	180.68	9.39	192.99	193.18	10.04
155.68	155.87	8.10	168.18	168.37	8.75	180.68	180.87	9.40	193.18	193.37	10.05
155.87	156.06	8.11	168.37	168.56	8.76	180.87	181.06	9.41	193.37	193.56	10.06
156.06	156.25	8.12	168.56	168.75	8.77	181.06	181.25	9.42	193.56	193.75	10.07
156.25	156.45	8.13	168.75	168.95	8.78	181.25	181.45	9.43	193.75	193.95	10.08
156.45	156.64	8.14	168.95	169.14	8.79	181.45	181.64	9.44	193.95	194.14	10.09
156.64	156.83	8.15	169.14	169.33	8.80	181.64	181.83	9.45	194.14	194.33	10.10
156.83	157.02	8.16	169.33	169.52	8.81	181.83	182.02	9.46	194.33	194.52	10.11
157.02	157.22	8.17	169.52	169.72	8.82	182.02	182.22	9.47	194.52	194.72	10.12
157.22	157.41	8.18	169.72	169.91	8.83	182.22	182.41	9.48	194.72	194.91	10.13
157.41	157.60	8.19	169.91	170.10	8.84	182.41	182.60	9.49	194.91	195.10	10.14
157.60	157.79	8.20	170.10	170.29	8.85	182.60	182.79	9.50	195.10	195.29	10.15
157.79	157.99	8.21	170.29	170.49	8.86	182.79	182.99	9.51	195.29	195.49	10.16
157.99	158.18	8.22	170.49	170.68	8.87	182.99	183.18	9.52	195.49	195.68	10.17
158.18	158.37	8.23	170.68	170.87	8.88	183.18	183.37	9.53	195.68	195.87	10.18
158.37	158.56	8.24	170.87	171.06	8.89	183.37	183.56	9.54	195.87	196.06	10.19
158.56	158.75	8.25	171.06	171.25	8.90	183.56	183.75	9.55	196.06	196.25	10.20
158.75	158.95	8.26	171.25	171.45	8.91	183.75	183.95	9.56	196.25	196.45	10.21
158.95	159.14	8.27	171.45	171.64	8.92	183.95	184.14	9.57	196.45	196.64	10.22
159.14	159.33	8.28	171.64	171.83	8.93	184.14	184.33	9.58	196.64	196.83	10.23
159.33	159.52	8.29	171.83	172.02	8.94	184.33	184.52	9.59	196.83	197.02	10.24
159.52	159.72	8.30	172.02	172.22	8.95	184.52	184.72	9.60	197.02	197.22	10.25
159.72	159.91	8.31	172.22	172.41	8.96	184.72	184.91	9.61	197.22	197.41	10.26
159.91	160.10	8.32	172.41	172.60	8.97	184.91	185.10	9.62	197.41	197.60	10.27
160.10	160.29	8.33	172.60	172.79	8.98	185.10	185.29	9.63	197.60	197.79	10.28
160.29	160.49	8.34	172.79	172.99	8.99	185.29	185.49	9.64	197.79	197.99	10.29
160.49	160.68	8.35	172.99	173.18	9.00	185.49	185.68	9.65	197.99	198.18	10.30
160.68	160.87	8.36	173.18	173.37	9.01	185.68	185.87	9.66	198.18	198.37	10.31
160.87	161.06	8.37	173.37	173.56	9.02	185.87	186.06	9.67	198.37	198.56	10.32
161.06	161.25	8.38	173.56	173.75	9.03	186.06	186.25	9.68	198.56	198.75	10.33
161.25	161.45	8.39	173.75	173.95	9.04	186.25	186.45	9.69	198.75	198.95	10.34
161.45	161.64	8.40	173.95	174.14	9.05	186.45	186.64	9.70	198.95	199.14	10.35
161.64	161.83	8.41	174.14	174.33	9.06	186.64	186.83	9.71	199.14	199.33	10.36
161.83	162.02	8.42	174.33	174.52	9.07	186.83	187.02	9.72	199.33	199.52	10.37
162.02	162.22	8.43	174.52	174.72	9.08	187.02	187.22	9.73	199.52	199.72	10.38
162.22	162.41	8.44	174.72	174.91	9.09	187.22	187.41	9.74	199.72	199.91	10.39

Social Security Employee Tax Table—Continued

5.2 percent employee tax deductions

Wages		Tax to be withheld	Wages		Tax to be withheld	Wages		Tax to be withheld	Wages		Tax to be withheld
At least	But less than		At least	But less than		At least	But less than		At least	But less than	
$199.91	$200.10	$10.40	$212.41	$212.60	$11.05	$224.91	$225.10	$11.70	$237.41	$237.60	$12.35
200.10	200.29	10.41	212.60	212.79	11.06	225.10	225.29	11.71	237.60	237.79	12.36
200.29	200.49	10.42	212.79	212.99	11.07	225.29	225.49	11.72	237.79	237.99	12.37
200.49	200.68	10.43	212.99	213.18	11.08	225.49	225.68	11.73	237.99	238.18	12.38
200.68	200.87	10.44	213.18	213.37	11.09	225.68	225.87	11.74	238.18	238.37	12.39
200.87	201.06	10.45	213.37	213.56	11.10	225.87	226.06	11.75	238.37	238.56	12.40
201.06	201.25	10.46	213.56	213.75	11.11	226.06	226.25	11.76	238.56	238.75	12.41
201.25	201.45	10.47	213.75	213.95	11.12	226.25	226.45	11.77	238.75	238.95	12.42
201.45	201.64	10.48	213.95	214.14	11.13	226.45	226.64	11.78	238.95	239.14	12.43
201.64	201.83	10.49	214.14	214.33	11.14	226.64	226.83	11.79	239.14	239.33	12.44
201.83	202.02	10.50	214.33	214.52	11.15	226.83	227.02	11.80	239.33	239.52	12.45
202.02	202.22	10.51	214.52	214.72	11.16	227.02	227.22	11.81	239.52	239.72	12.46
202.22	202.41	10.52	214.72	214.91	11.17	227.22	227.41	11.82	239.72	239.91	12.47
202.41	202.60	10.53	214.91	215.10	11.18	227.41	227.60	11.83	239.91	240.10	12.48
202.60	202.79	10.54	215.10	215.29	11.19	227.60	227.79	11.84	240.10	240.29	12.49
202.79	202.99	10.55	215.29	215.49	11.20	227.79	227.99	11.85	240.29	240.49	12.50
202.99	203.18	10.56	215.49	215.68	11.21	227.99	228.18	11.86	240.49	240.68	12.51
203.18	203.37	10.57	215.68	215.87	11.22	228.18	228.37	11.87	240.68	240.87	12.52
203.37	203.56	10.58	215.87	216.06	11.23	228.37	228.56	11.88	240.87	241.06	12.53
203.56	203.75	10.59	216.06	216.25	11.24	228.56	228.75	11.89	241.06	241.25	12.54
203.75	203.95	10.60	216.25	216.45	11.25	228.75	228.95	11.90	241.25	241.45	12.55
203.95	204.14	10.61	216.45	216.64	11.26	228.95	229.14	11.91	241.45	241.64	12.56
204.14	204.33	10.62	216.64	216.83	11.27	229.14	229.33	11.92	241.64	241.83	12.57
204.33	204.52	10.63	216.83	217.02	11.28	229.33	229.52	11.93	241.83	242.02	12.58
204.52	204.72	10.64	217.02	217.22	11.29	229.52	229.72	11.94	242.02	242.22	12.59
204.72	204.91	10.65	217.22	217.41	11.30	229.72	229.91	11.95	242.22	242.41	12.60
204.91	205.10	10.66	217.41	217.60	11.31	229.91	230.10	11.96	242.41	242.60	12.61
205.10	205.29	10.67	217.60	217.79	11.32	230.10	230.29	11.97	242.60	242.79	12.62
205.29	205.49	10.68	217.79	217.99	11.33	230.29	230.49	11.98	242.79	242.99	12.63
205.49	205.68	10.69	217.99	218.18	11.34	230.49	230.68	11.99	242.99	243.18	12.64
205.68	205.87	10.70	218.18	218.37	11.35	230.68	230.87	12.00	243.18	243.37	12.65
205.87	206.06	10.71	218.37	218.56	11.36	230.87	231.06	12.01	243.37	243.56	12.66
206.06	206.25	10.72	218.56	218.75	11.37	231.06	231.25	12.02	243.56	243.75	12.67
206.25	206.45	10.73	218.75	218.95	11.38	231.25	231.45	12.03	243.75	243.95	12.68
206.45	206.64	10.74	218.95	219.14	11.39	231.45	231.64	12.04	243.95	244.14	12.69
206.64	206.83	10.75	219.14	219.33	11.40	231.64	231.83	12.05	244.14	244.33	12.70
206.83	207.02	10.76	219.33	219.52	11.41	231.83	232.02	12.06	244.33	244.52	12.71
207.02	207.22	10.77	219.52	219.72	11.42	232.02	232.22	12.07	244.52	244.72	12.72
207.22	207.41	10.78	219.72	219.91	11.43	232.22	232.41	12.08	244.72	244.91	12.73
207.41	207.60	10.79	219.91	220.10	11.44	232.41	232.60	12.09	244.91	245.10	12.74
207.60	207.79	10.80	220.10	220.29	11.45	232.60	232.79	12.10	245.10	245.29	12.75
207.79	207.99	10.81	220.29	220.49	11.46	232.79	232.99	12.11	245.29	245.49	12.76
207.99	208.18	10.82	220.49	220.68	11.47	232.99	233.18	12.12	245.49	245.68	12.77
208.18	208.37	10.83	220.68	220.87	11.48	233.18	233.37	12.13	245.68	245.87	12.78
208.37	208.56	10.84	220.87	221.06	11.49	233.37	233.56	12.14	245.87	246.06	12.79
208.56	208.75	10.85	221.06	221.25	11.50	233.56	233.75	12.15	246.06	246.25	12.80
208.75	208.95	10.86	221.25	221.45	11.51	233.75	233.95	12.16	246.25	246.45	12.81
208.95	209.14	10.87	221.45	221.64	11.52	233.95	234.14	12.17	246.45	246.64	12.82
209.14	209.33	10.88	221.64	221.83	11.53	234.14	234.33	12.18	246.64	246.83	12.83
209.33	209.52	10.89	221.83	222.02	11.54	234.33	234.52	12.19	246.83	247.02	12.84
209.52	209.72	10.90	222.02	222.22	11.55	234.52	234.72	12.20	247.02	247.22	12.85
209.72	209.91	10.91	222.22	222.41	11.56	234.72	234.91	12.21	247.22	247.41	12.86
209.91	210.10	10.92	222.41	222.60	11.57	234.91	235.10	12.22	247.41	247.60	12.87
210.10	210.29	10.93	222.60	222.79	11.58	235.10	235.29	12.23	247.60	247.79	12.88
210.29	210.49	10.94	222.79	222.99	11.59	235.29	235.49	12.24	247.79	247.99	12.89
210.49	210.68	10.95	222.99	223.18	11.60	235.49	235.68	12.25	247.99	248.18	12.90
210.68	210.87	10.96	223.18	223.37	11.61	235.68	235.87	12.26	248.18	248.37	12.91
210.87	211.06	10.97	223.37	223.56	11.62	235.87	236.06	12.27	248.37	248.56	12.92
211.06	211.25	10.98	223.56	223.75	11.63	236.06	236.25	12.28	248.56	248.75	12.93
211.25	211.45	10.99	223.75	223.95	11.64	236.25	236.45	12.29	248.75	248.95	12.94
211.45	211.64	11.00	223.95	224.14	11.65	236.45	236.64	12.30	248.95	249.14	12.95
211.64	211.83	11.01	224.14	224.33	11.66	236.64	236.83	12.31	249.14	249.33	12.96
211.83	212.02	11.02	224.33	224.52	11.67	236.83	237.02	12.32	249.33	249.52	12.97
212.02	212.22	11.03	224.52	224.72	11.68	237.02	237.22	12.33	249.52	249.72	12.98
212.22	212.41	11.04	224.72	224.91	11.69	237.22	237.41	12.34	249.72	249.91	12.99

FIGURE 5.3. (Continued.)

WEEKLY WITHHOLDING TAX TABLE

WAGES		EXEMPTIONS CLAIMED										
At Least	Less Than	0	1	2	3	4	5	6	7	8	9	10 or more
						TAX TO BE WITHHELD						
$ 0	$ 27	$ .00										
27	28	.00										
28	29	.00										
29	30	.10										
30	31	.10										
31	32	.10										
32	33	.20										
33	34	.20										
34	35	.20										
35	36	.30										
36	37	.30										
37	38	.30										
38	39	.30										
39	40	.40										
40	41	.40										
41	42	.40										
42	43	.40	.10									
43	44	.50	.10									
44	45	.50	.10									
45	46	.50	.10									
46	47	.50	.20									
47	48	.60	.20									
48	49	.60	.20									
49	50	.60	.30									
50	51	.60	.30	.10								
51	52	.70	.30	.10								
52	53	.70	.30	.10								
53	54	.70	.40	.10								
54	55	.70	.40	.20	.10							
55	56	.80	.40	.20	.10							
56	57	.80	.50	.20	.10							
57	58	.80	.50	.30	.10							
58	59	.90	.50	.30	.20	.10						
59	60	.90	.60	.30	.20	.10						
60	62	.90	.60	.40	.20	.10						
62	64	1.00	.60	.40	.30	.10						
64	66	1.00	.70	.50	.30	.10						
66	68	1.10	.70	.50	.40	.10						
68	70	1.10	.80	.60	.40	.20						
70	72	1.20	.80	.60	.40	.20						
72	74	1.30	.90	.60	.50	.30	.10					
74	76	1.30	.90	.70	.50	.30	.10					
76	78	1.40	1.00	.70	.60	.40	.10					
78	80	1.50	1.00	.80	.60	.40	.20					
80	82	1.60	1.10	.80	.60	.50	.30	.10				
82	84	1.60	1.20	.90	.70	.50	.30	.10				
84	86	1.70	1.20	1.00	.70	.60	.40	.10				
86	88	1.80	1.30	1.00	.80	.60	.40	.20				
88	90	1.80	1.40	1.10	.80	.60	.50	.30	.10			
90	92	1.90	1.40	1.10	.90	.70	.50	.30	.10			
92	94	2.00	1.50	1.20	.90	.70	.60	.40	.10			
94	96	2.10	1.60	1.20	1.00	.80	.60	.40	.20			
96	98	2.10	1.60	1.30	1.00	.80	.60	.50	.30	.10		
98	100	2.20	1.70	1.30	1.10	.80	.70	.50	.30	.10		
100	105	2.30	1.80	1.40	1.20	.90	.70	.60	.40	.20		

WAGES		EXEMPTIONS CLAIMED										
At Least	Less Than	0	1	2	3	4	5	6	7	8	9	10 or more
						TAX TO BE WITHHELD						
$ 105	$ 110	$ 2.50	$ 2.00	$ 1.50	$ 1.00	$ .70	$ .30					
110	115	2.70	2.20	1.70	1.20	.80	.40	.10				
115	120	2.90	2.40	1.90	1.40	.90	.60	.20				
120	125	3.10	2.50	2.00	1.60	1.10	.70	.30				
125	130	3.30	2.70	2.20	1.70	1.20	.80	.50	.10			
130	135	3.60	2.90	2.40	1.90	1.40	1.00	.60	.20			
135	140	3.80	3.20	2.60	2.10	1.60	1.10	.70	.40	.10		
140	145	4.00	3.40	2.80	2.20	1.80	1.30	.90	.50	.30		
145	150	4.20	3.60	3.00	2.40	1.90	1.40	1.00	.60	.30	.10	
150	160	4.50	3.90	3.30	2.70	2.20	1.70	1.20	.80	.40	.30	.20
160	170	5.10	4.40	3.60	3.10	2.50	2.00	1.60	1.10	.70	.60	.50
170	180	5.60	4.80	4.20	3.60	3.00	2.40	1.90	1.40	1.00	.60	.80
180	190	6.10	5.40	4.60	4.00	3.40	2.80	2.30	1.80	1.30	.90	1.00
190	200	6.60	5.90	5.20	4.40	3.80	3.20	2.60	2.10	1.60	1.20	1.40
200	210	7.20	6.40	5.70	5.00	4.20	3.60	3.10	2.50	2.00	1.50	1.70
210	220	7.80	7.00	6.20	5.50	4.70	4.10	3.50	2.90	2.30	1.80	2.10
220	230	8.40	7.60	6.70	6.00	5.30	4.50	3.90	3.30	2.70	2.20	2.40
230	240	9.00	8.20	7.30	6.50	5.80	5.10	4.40	3.70	3.10	2.50	2.80
240	250	9.60	8.80	7.90	7.10	6.30	5.60	4.80	4.20	3.60	3.00	3.20
250	260	10.30	9.40	8.50	7.70	6.80	6.10	5.40	4.60	4.00	3.40	3.70
260	270	11.00	10.10	9.10	8.30	7.40	6.60	5.90	5.20	4.40	3.80	4.10
270	280	11.70	10.80	9.80	8.90	8.00	7.20	6.40	5.70	5.00	4.30	4.50
280	290	12.40	11.50	10.50	9.50	8.70	7.80	7.00	6.20	5.50	4.70	5.10
290	300	13.20	12.20	11.20	10.20	9.30	8.40	7.60	6.70	6.00	5.30	5.60
300	310	14.00	12.90	11.90	10.90	9.90	9.00	8.20	7.30	6.50	5.80	6.10
310	320	14.80	13.70	12.60	11.60	10.60	9.60	8.80	7.90	7.10	6.30	6.60
320	330	15.50	14.40	13.40	12.30	11.30	10.30	9.40	8.50	7.70	6.80	7.20
330	340	16.40	15.20	14.10	13.00	12.00	11.00	10.10	9.10	8.30	7.40	7.80
340	350	17.20	16.00	14.90	13.80	12.70	11.70	10.80	9.80	8.90	8.00	8.40
350	360	18.10	16.90	15.70	14.60	13.50	12.50	11.50	10.50	9.50	8.70	9.00
360	370	19.00	17.70	16.50	15.40	14.30	13.20	12.20	11.20	10.20	9.30	9.60
370	380	19.80	18.60	17.40	16.20	15.10	14.00	12.90	11.90	10.90	9.90	10.30
380	390	20.80	19.50	18.30	17.10	15.90	14.80	13.70	12.60	11.60	10.60	9.60
390	400	21.70	20.40	19.10	17.90	16.70	15.50	14.40	13.40	12.30	11.30	10.30
400	410	22.70	21.40	20.00	18.80	17.60	16.40	15.20	14.10	13.00	12.00	11.00
410	420	23.70	22.30	21.00	19.70	18.40	17.20	16.00	14.90	13.80	12.70	11.70
420	430	24.70	23.30	21.90	20.60	19.30	18.10	16.90	15.70	14.60	13.50	12.40
430	440	25.70	24.20	22.80	21.60	20.20	19.00	17.70	16.50	15.40	14.10	13.10
440	450	26.70	25.20	23.80	22.50	21.10	19.80	18.60	17.30	16.20	15.10	14.80
450	460	27.80	26.30	24.80	23.40	22.10	20.80	19.50	18.30	17.10	15.90	15.50
460	470	28.80	27.40	25.90	24.40	23.10	21.70	20.40	19.10	18.00	16.70	16.40
470	480	30.00	28.60	27.00	25.50	24.00	22.70	21.40	20.00	18.80	17.60	17.20
480	490	31.10	29.70	28.20	26.50	25.10	23.80	22.30	21.00	19.70	18.40	18.10
490	500	32.20	30.90	29.30	27.60	26.10	24.90	23.50	22.10	20.80	19.30	19.00
500	510	33.40	31.80	30.20	28.60	27.20	25.70	24.20	22.90	21.60	20.20	19.80
510	520	34.60	32.90	31.30	29.70	28.20	26.70	25.30	23.80	22.50	21.10	20.80
520	530	35.80	34.10	32.50	30.90	29.30	27.80	26.30	24.90	23.50	22.10	21.70
530	540	37.00	35.30	33.60	32.00	30.40	28.80	27.40	25.90	24.40	23.10	22.70
540	550	38.20	36.50	34.80	33.10	31.60	30.00	28.40	27.00	25.50	24.00	23.70
550	560	39.40	37.70	36.00	34.30	32.70	31.10	29.50	28.00	26.50	25.10	24.70
560	570	40.60	38.90	37.20	35.50	33.80	32.20	30.70	29.10	27.60	26.10	25.70
570	580	41.90	40.20	38.50	36.70	35.00	33.40	31.80	30.20	28.60	27.20	26.70
580	590	43.10	41.40	39.70	38.00	36.30	34.60	32.90	31.30	29.70	28.20	27.80
590	600	44.30	42.60	40.90	39.20	37.50	35.80	34.10	32.50	30.90	29.30	28.30
600 & over		44.90	43.20	41.50	39.80	38.10	36.40	34.70	33.00	31.40	29.90	28.30

+ 12.18% of excess over $600

FIGURE 5.4. TAX TABLES FOR STATE TAX.

Let us assume that the total deductions from Joan's salary are as follows:

Withholding tax	$10.70
Social security tax	5.93
N.Y. State income tax	1.70
Total deductions	$18.33

Net Pay

Net pay is determined by subtracting deductions from gross pay and is calculated for Joan as follows:

Gross pay	$101.00
— Deductions	18.33
Net Pay	$ 82.67

Recapping Our Work

Joan's pay is determined as follows:

Gross pay		$101.00
Value of tips	+	10.00
Pay for purposes of federal and state withholding tax	=	$111.00
Value of room and board	+	3.00
Pay for social security purposes	=	$114.00
Deductions:		
Federal withholding tax	$10.70	
Social Security Tax	5.93	
New York State Tax	1.70	
Total Deductions	$18.33	
Gross pay		$101.00
Total deductions	—	18.33
Net pay		$ 82.67

AN ALTERNATIVE WAY OF DETERMINING DEDUCTIBLE AMOUNTS

Some employers will not choose to use the tax tables as provided or cannot use them because there is no tax table for the particular circumstance of the employee. For example, there is no table for an

Tables for Percentage Method of Withholding

TABLE 1. WEEKLY Payroll Period

(a) SINGLE person—including head of household:

If the amount of wages is:		The amount of income tax to be withheld shall be:	
Not over $20		0	
Over—	But not over—		of excess over—
$20	—$31	14%	—$20
$31	—$50	$1.54 plus 17%	—$31
$50	—$100	$4.77 plus 20%	—$50
$100	—$135	$14.77 plus 18%	—$100
$135	—$212	$21.07 plus 21%	—$135
$212		$37.24 plus 24%	—$212

(b) MARRIED person—

If the amount of wages is:		The amount of income tax to be withheld shall be:	
Not over $20		0	
Over—	But not over—		of excess over—
$20	—$42	14%	—$20
$42	—$77	$3.08 plus 17%	—$42
$77	—$163	$9.03 plus 16%	—$77
$163	—$269	$22.79 plus 19%	—$163
$269	—$385	$42.93 plus 21%	—$269
$385		$67.29 plus 25%	—$385

Weekly	$12.50
Biweekly	25.00
Semimonthly	27.10
Monthly	54.20
Quarterly	162.50
Semiannual	325.00
Annual	650.00
Daily or miscellaneous (per day of such period)	1.80

FIGURE 5.5.   TAX TABLES FOR WITHHOLDING TAX USING THE PERCENTAGE METHOD.

employee who is paid every other month. The Internal Revenue Service provides us with an alternative way of computing deductible amounts for withholding tax. It is called the percentage method (Figure 5.5). The steps in the computation are as follows: [1]

1. Multiply the amount of one withholding exemption (see Figure 5.5) by the number of exemptions claimed by the employee;
2. Subtract the amount thus determined from the employee's wages;
3. Determine amount to be withheld from appropriate table.

Joan's federal withholding tax would be calculated as follows:

1. Two exemptions $\times$ $12.50 = $25.
2. $111 - $25 = $86.
3. $9.03 (from Figure 5.5) + 16 percent of the excess over $77 ($86 - $77 = $9). 16 percent of $9 = $1.44. Amount to be deducted is $9.03 + $1.44 = $10.47.

The above method requires a considerable amount of calculation and would ordinarily not be used. However, many payrolls are computerized, and the above system can be programmed into the computer with the computer doing all the calculations.

Social security tax can also be computed without the tax tables. A straight percent (it is presently about 5 percent) is taken from the pay for social security purposes.

INDIVIDUAL PAYROLL RECORD

All of the previous pay determinations are calculated on the *employee's personal record* (Figure 5.6). We maintain an individual payroll record for each of our employees. The record is divided into quarters, two on the front side and two on the back side. At the end of each quarter of a year (March 31, June 30, September 30, and December 31) the employer must prepare a quarterly report indicating how much he has deducted from all employees, and he must list each employee's name and the amount deducted. The employee's personal record is set up in such a fashion that the employer can readily add the pay and deductions from each pay period to obtain the required information for the quarterly report.

At the top of each individual record is a recap portion. The information from each quarter is put in that part of the record and added to determine the amount withheld and total wages for the year.

[1] Internal Revenue Service Employers Tax Guide

EMPLOYEE'S PERSONAL RECORD

TRANSPORTATION ☐ FEE ☐ FEMALE   DEPT. _Housekeeping_

OCCUPATION _Maid_   AGE _36_

NAME _Joan Turner_

S.S. NO. _005-30-5067_

DATE BEGAN _6/1_ @ $ ____ PER _hr._

ADDRESS _Box 252_
Plainville, N.Y.

DATE ENDED ____

REMARKS ____

NO. OF EXEMPTIONS _2_ S.–IF SINGLE _M_–IF MARRIED _M_   STUDENT ☐

W-2 RECAP

	FED. W. TAX 7	TOTAL WAGES FOR FED W TAX 3	TOTAL WAGES FOR FED. S.S. 5	S.S. TAX WITHHELD 6	STATE TAX WITHHELD 8	CITY TAX WITHHELD 9
1ST Q.						
2ND Q.	25 30	331 –	340 –	17 71	370	
3RD Q.						
4TH Q.						
TOTAL						

_2nd_ QUARTER

FOR PERIOD ENDING	HOURS WORKED 1	2	3	4	5	6	7	WEEKLY TOTAL REG. O.T	✓	EARNINGS 1 SALARY	2 TIPS	3 TOTAL WAGES FOR W. TAX	4 MEALS & LODGING	5 TOTAL FOR S.S. & U.I.	6 FED. S.S.	7 FED. W. TAX	8 STATE W. TAX	9 CITY W. TAX	DEDUCTIONS DIS. INS.	AGENCY	MISC.	TOTAL DEDUCT.	NET PAY	PAYMENTS DATE	FOLIO	AMOUNT	✓
6/7	8	9	10	8	8	9	4	40 7		101 –	10 –	111 –	43 –	119 –	5 83	10 70	1 70				18 23	82 67	6/7	325	82 67	
6/14	8	8	8	8	8	1		40 1		83 –	10 –	93 –	2 50	95 50	4 99	7 50	1 –				13 49	69 51	6/14	420	69 51	
6/21	8	8	8	9	8	8		40		80 –	10 –	90 –	2 50	92 50	4 81	7 10	1 –				12 91	67 09	6/21	580	67 09	
6/28	8	8						16		32 –	5 –	37 –	1 –	38 –	1 98						1 98	30 02	6/28	730	30 02	
										296 – 35		331 –	9 –	396 –	17 71	25 30	3 70					46 71	249 29			249 29	

_____ QUARTER

FIGURE 5.6. EMPLOYEE'S PERSONAL RECORD.

The recap portion will be used as information for the annual W-2 form (Figure 5.7) sent to each employee and to the federal government. The W-2 form is used by each of us as a basis for figuring our annual federal income tax.

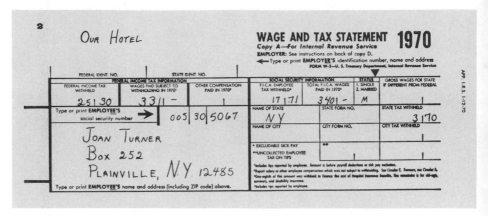

FIGURE 5.7.   W-2 FORM WAGE AND TAX STATEMENT.

THE PAYROLL JOURNAL

After the accounting department has determined the pay of each of the hotel's employees, the information is transferred to a *payroll journal*. The employees' individual payroll records are separated and listed by department in units. We list them on the payroll journal that way because we will later want to have information about the payroll expenses of each department. Figure 5.8 illustrates a payroll journal completed for one payroll period.

The journal is added and balanced in much the same fashion as our transcript of guest ledger (Figure 5.9). The total of columns 1 and 2 must equal the sum of column 3. Columns 3 and 4 must equal column 5. The sum of the deduction column must equal the total deductions column. And column 1 minus the total deductions column must equal the net pay column. Can you determine why?

We are reasonably sure that each of the paychecks is mathematically correct when we have balanced our payroll journal, and we will then write the paychecks. Payroll checks are not written until our payroll journal is balanced because we do not want to take the chance that one or more of the checks is incorrect. Some employers have foolishly allowed checks to be written and distributed prior to the balancing of the payroll journal and later found that a sizable error was made in one or more checks. In more than one instance, the employee has cashed his check and left town before he could be caught.

Most hotels have a separate bank account and separate checks for payroll because of the large number of checks written. Only the amount needed for the payroll will be deposited in the payroll account. This system facilitates the verification of the payroll with actual checks cashed and reduces the number of checks going through our regular checking account.

A MEANS OF REDUCING THE WORK IN COMPUTING PAYROLL

In the previous illustration of payroll computation, we had to go through three different processes for each check. The individual payroll record was computed, this information was transferred to the payroll journal, and a payroll check listing essentially the same information was written for the employee. The effort expended each week in a hotel with a large number of employees just to determine payroll is burdensome at best. Thus, several ways of reducing this work have come into being.

The first of these is a manual method that does essentially what we have previously described. However, instead of there being three different steps, there is only one. The individual payroll record and payroll check are printed with carbon paper attached. A figure written once is inscribed on all three records. The individual payroll record is placed over the payroll journal on the correct line, and the check is placed over the individual payroll record. The accountant then determines the pay of each employee while writing directly on the check. His figures are transposed to the other two records by the carbon paper.

The second method uses the same basic procedure as above, except that an accounting machine is used to do all the calculations and a typewriter is used by the operator to write the name of the employee onto the check. The machine gives us totals of the payroll journal, saving a great deal of adding and balancing. The NCR Class 33 is an example of one of these machines. It has the advantage of being able to calculate more rapidly and accurately than the human brain, and the work is much neater because everything is in typewritten form.

In larger hotels a computer is used to compute payroll. Each employee's name, social security number, exemptions, and rate of pay is programmed into the computer, and the computer retains this informa-

S.S. no.	Name	Times Pay / Worked Overtime	1 Salary	2 Tips	3 Total wages for w. tax	4 Meals an lodging
	Rooms Dept.					
005 305 067	Joan Turner	40 7	101 —	10 —	111 —	3
003 427 615	Mary Jones	40 10	110 —	15 —	125 —	3
005 304 029	Paul Fox	40	125 —		125 —	2
003 647 235	James Jackson	40	100 —		100 —	2
004 677 765	Jane Temple	40	90 —		90 —	2
	Total rooms dept		526 —	25 —	551 —	13
	Food and Beverage					
207 632 573	John Timpone	40	150 —		150 —	2
033 624 620	Jerry Bianco	40 5	160 —		160 —	2
005 304 277	Peter Blum	40	40 —	60 —	100 —	2
003 403 277	Bruce Amble	40	40 —	65 —	105 —	2
	Total food and beverage		390 —	125 —	515 —	10
	Administrative					
076 446 622	Bill Manner		250 —		250 —	3
066 324 266	Beth Brody	40	100 —		100 —	2
	Total administrative		350 —		350 —	5
	Total all Departments		1266 —	150 —	1416 —	29
					✓	
					=	
			Debit	1266 -		
			wages	+ 150 -		
			expense	1416 00		
			#550	+ 29 00		
				1445 00		
						1266
						248
						1017

FIGURE 5.8.   PAYROLL JOURNAL.

		Deductions						
=5=	=6=	=7=	=8=	=9=	=10=	=11=	=12=	
Total for s. s.	Federal s. s.	Federal w. tax	State w. tax		Total deductions	Net pay	Check no	
								1
114 -	593	10 70	1 70		18 33	82 67		2
128 -	666	13 10	2 70		22 46	87 54		3
127 50	663	11 10	2 20		19 93	105 07		4
102 50	533	7 -	90		13 23	86 77		5
92 50	481	5 -	60		10 41	79 59		6
564 50	29 36	46 90	8 10		84 36	441 64		7
								8
								9
152 50	7 93	17 50	3 30		28 73	121 27		10
162 50	8 45	19 10	3 10		30 65	129 35		11
102 50	5 33	9 10	1 80		16 23	23 77		12
107 50	5 59	9 90	1 00		16 49	23 51		13
525 -	27 30	55 60	9 20		92 10	297 90		14
								15
								16
253 -	13 16	35 50	8 50		57 16	192 84		17
102 50	5 33	9 10	90		15 33	84 67		18
355 50	18 49	44 60	9 40		72 49	277 51		19
								20
1445 -	75 15	147 10	26 70		248 95	1017 05		21
								22
								23
	Credit	Credit	Credit	75 15	=		Credit	24
	s. s. tax	w. tax	state tax	147 10			wages	25
	payable	payable	payable	26 70			payable	26
	#212	#211	#213	248 95			#202	27

SHEET NO. _____

ACCOUNT NO. _202_

TERMS

NAME _Wages Payable_

RATING

ADDRESS

CREDIT LIMIT

DATE 19	ITEMS	FOLIO	✓	DEBITS	DATE 19	ITEMS	FOLIO	✓	CREDITS
					June 7		P.J		1017 05

SHEET NO. _____

ACCOUNT NO. _211_

TERMS

NAME _Federal Withholding Taxes Payable_

RATING

ADDRESS

CREDIT LIMIT

DATE 19	ITEMS	FOLIO	✓	DEBITS	DATE 19	ITEMS	FOLIO	✓	CREDITS
					June 7		P.J		147 10

SHEET NO. _____

ACCOUNT NO. _212_

TERMS

NAME _Social Security Taxes Payable_

RATING

ADDRESS

CREDIT LIMIT

DATE 19	ITEMS	FOLIO	✓	DEBITS	DATE 19	ITEMS	FOLIO	✓	CREDITS
					June 7		P.J		75 15

SHEET NO. _____

ACCOUNT NO. _213_

TERMS

NAME _State Tax Payable_

RATING

ADDRESS

CREDIT LIMIT

DATE 19	ITEMS	FOLIO	✓	DEBITS	DATE 19	ITEMS	FOLIO	✓	CREDITS
					June 7		P.J		26 70

SHEET NO. _____

ACCOUNT NO. _550_

TERMS

NAME _Wages Expense_

RATING

ADDRESS

CREDIT LIMIT

DATE 19	ITEMS	FOLIO	✓	DEBITS	DATE 19	ITEMS	FOLIO	✓	CREDITS
June 7		P.J		1266 —					

FIGURE 5.9. LEDGER ACCOUNT FOR PAYROLL JOURNAL.

tion from week to week. The total hours worked for each employee is given to the computer each week, and it automatically computes pay, keeps individual payroll records, prepares the payroll journal totals, and prints out the payroll check.

POSTING TO THE GENERAL LEDGER ACCOUNTS

We will post from our payroll journal to the general ledger accounts each week, or we will prepare a summary and post only monthly. Whichever method we choose, the posting procedure will be the same.

The total salary column will be posted as a debit to wages expense, since that is our actual payroll cost. The offsetting credit entries will be to federal withholding tax payable, state tax payable, social security tax payable, and payroll payable—all liability accounts.

When the liability accounts are paid, we will debit them and credit cash through the cash disbursements journal explained in the next chapter. The payroll payable account will be debited through the cash disbursements journal immediately, because we will need to write a check to our payroll account to cover the individual payroll checks issued to employees. The remaining liabilities are not due immediately, so we will not pay them now. A "deposit" of these liabilities will be made to the treasury periodically, and any balance owed will be made when the quarterly report is filed.

SUMMARY

Legislation enacted by the federal government and most state governments requires employers to pay all employees a minimum wage and extra pay for overtime.

Most hotels provide room and board for employees when their hours of work overlap the meal hours or when room is a necessary part of an employee's job. Pay for those employees is calculated by the following formula:

$$\begin{array}{r} \text{Gross Wages} \\ -\ \textit{Deductions} \\ \hline = \text{Net Pay} \end{array}$$

The amount to be deducted for state and federal withholding tax is determined by the federal and state tax tables. We add declared tips to gross wages to determine the tax base for deducting withholding tax.

Social security tax is also derived from the tax tables. However, we must add the value of room and board to the withholding tax base to determine a tax base for social security tax.

Other deductions are sometimes made from employees' pay. These include employee contributions to retirement, union dues, advances on salary, and health insurance premiums.

The amount to be paid to each employee is first determined on the employee's individual payroll record. That information is transferred to the payroll journal, and finally a paycheck is written. In recent years methods have been devised to eliminate the need for three separate steps in the computation of pay. One method uses carbon paper so that a figure written once is transposed to all three records. Another method employs the use of a calculator with a built in typewriter. A third method utilizes a computer to determine pay, prepare the necessary records, and print the payroll check.

QUESTIONS FOR DISCUSSION

1. Determine the pay for Joan using the alternative method of pay where room and board are deducted from salary.
2. Present a forceful argument in favor of a minimum wage for all hotel employees. What could you say to counteract the argument that higher wages cause hotels to employ fewer people and thus cause service to deteriorate?
3. What advantages are there to the hotel's having a biweekly payroll period as opposed to a semimonthly payroll period?
4. Explain the importance of the hotel's maintaining departmental time records for employees in addition to the time card.
5. If an employee does not declare all his tips, do you think Internal Revenue can catch him? Why?
6. The amount of withholding tax deducted from Joan's salary is more using the percentage method. Does that mean that Joan will actually pay more taxes than she should when she files her income tax form?
7. Explain why total wages as listed on the W-2 form might be shown as two different figures. When would the two figures be the same?

6 | Accounting for Cash Disbursements

The last subsidiary journals we will discuss involve the payment of cash. Just as we need special journals to handle cash receipts, we also need special journals for cash disbursements because of the many checks we will write over the financial period.

Actually, we will need two journals for the disbursement of cash. One will take care of the many minor purchases we make and pay cash for, and the other will take care of the checks we will write from our bank account. We will first discuss the one used to pay our bills by check.

THE CASH DISBURSEMENTS JOURNAL

Bills we receive are first recorded in our purchase journal. You will recall that the journal was added, and the amounts were posted to the ledger accounts at the end of the month. The total amount of our purchases was posted as a credit to accounts payable. The individual amounts for each of our creditors were posted to the accounts payable subsidiary ledger.

When bills are paid, we will credit our cash account and debit accounts payable to show decreases in cash and accounts payable. The journal used to record these transactions is the *cash disbursements journal* illustrated in Figure 6.1. It has several columns in need of explanation. The amount column will be posted as a credit to the cash account. The cash discount column will also be posted as a credit. It

Cash Disbursements Journal

Credits

	Date	Paid to	Check no.	Amount (1)	Cash discount (2)	Accounts payable (3) (4)
1	June 1	Petty Cash	1222	200 -		
2	1	Masey Furniture	1223	760 -		
3	5	Allen Meats	1224	47 48	97	48 4
4	5	Quick Meats	1225	43 12	88	44
5	5	Max Repairs	1226	25 -		25
6	6	Petty Cash	1227	55 -		
7	7	Shell Fuel	1228	120 -		1 20
8	7	Payroll Account	1229	990 88		
9				2241 48	1 85	237 -
10						
11						
12				2241 48	237 45	
13				1 85	990 88	
14					255 -	
15					760 -	
16				2243 33	2243 33	
17				Credit Cash	Credit Cash	Debit accounts
18						
19				Cash	discount	payable
20				# 100		
21					# 507	# 201
22						
23						

FIGURE 6.1. CASH DISBURSEMENTS JOURNAL.

will be posted to the cash discount ledger account, a negative expense account. When goods were purchased, we entered the full amount of the invoices in our purchase journal. Many of the invoices entitle us to a cash discount for paying the bill within a short period of time. Most food bills will let us deduct 1 or 2 percent from the total amount

Debits								
≡5≡	≡6≡	≡7≡	≡8≡	≡9≡	≡10≡	≡11≡	≡12≡	
Payroll payable	*Petty cash*	*Sundries* *amount*	*detail*					
	200 -							1
		760 -	*Purchase new*					2
			furniture					3
								4
								5
	55 -							6
								7
990 88								8
990 88	255 -	760 -						9
								10
								11
								12
								13
								14
								15
								16
Debit	*Debit*	*Debit*						17
payroll	*petty*	*furniture*						18
payable	*cash*	*and fixtures*						19
#202	#101	#171						20
								21
								22

if they are paid within ten days. However, we have already credited the full amount of the bills to accounts payable. So, in order to show the full payment, we must debit it for the full amount. Thus, we debit the account for the full amount of the bill, credit cash for the amount we are paying, and credit cash discount for the amount of the discount we receive. The cash discount ledger account will be deducted from our expenses when determining profit.

The remainder of the accounts will be posted as debits. The accounts payable column will be posted as a debit to that account to show a decrease in the amount owed. The payroll column will be posted as a debit to payroll payable. You will recall that we set up the payroll as a liability account from the payroll journal. We now are showing that amount is no longer owed. The petty cash column is used when we write checks to our petty cash bank (petty cash is used to purchase incidental items for cash). The sundries column is very important in the cash disbursements journal because it is used when we write a check that is not already set up as an account payable. Another way of saying the same thing is that the sundries column is used for all bills or purchases that were not first run through the purchase journal. We post directly to the asset or expense account from this column.

We now have two ways of handling purchases. We can (1) post them to the purchase journal and thereby debit the expense or asset and credit acounts payable. And when we pay the bill, we will credit cash and debit accounts payable. Or we can (2) immediately write a check and, using the sundries column, credit cash and debit the asset or expense. These two methods are illustrated below for the purchase of $100 worth of housekeeping supplies.

Using the purchase journal and cash disbursements journal:

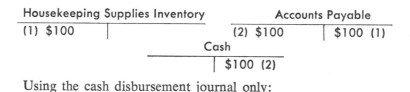

Using the cash disbursement journal only:

Housekeeping Supplies Inventory   Cash
$100 | | $100

You might, at this point, ask why we use a purchase journal at all if it involves an extra bookkeeping step. The answer is that it saves us clutter in the ledger accounts (Figure 6.2). In addition the purchase journal provides us with a means of recognizing an expense or purchase immediately, even if we do not wish to pay the bill now.

At or about the same time the person recording entries to our cash disbursements journal is writing in the various entries, he will also post as debits to the accounts payable subsidiary ledger accounts the amounts

FIGURE 6.2.   LEDGER ACCOUNTS FOR CASH DISBURSEMENTS JOURNAL.

SHEET NO. _____ ACCOUNT NO. 201

TERMS NAME Accounts Payable Control
RATING ADDRESS
CREDIT LIMIT

DATE 19	ITEMS	FOLIO	/	DEBITS	DATE 19	ITEMS	FOLIO	/	CREDITS
June 7		CD		237 45	June 4	207.80	PJ		445 25

SHEET NO. _____ ACCOUNT NO. 222

TERMS NAME Allen Meats
RATING ADDRESS
CREDIT LIMIT

DATE 19	ITEMS	FOLIO	/	DEBITS	DATE 19	ITEMS	FOLIO	/	CREDITS
June 5				48 45	June 2				35 75
					4	11			23 70
									59 75

SHEET NO. _____ ACCOUNT NO. 232

TERMS NAME Quick Meats Inc.
RATING ADDRESS
CREDIT LIMIT

DATE 19	ITEMS	FOLIO	/	DEBITS	DATE 19	ITEMS	FOLIO	/	CREDITS
June 5				44 —	June 2				44 —

SHEET NO. _____ ACCOUNT NO. 233

TERMS NAME Max Repairs
RATING ADDRESS
CREDIT LIMIT

DATE 19	ITEMS	FOLIO	/	DEBITS	DATE 19	ITEMS	FOLIO	/	CREDITS
June 5				25 —	June 2				25 —
					4	30			30 —
									55 —

SHEET NO. _____ ACCOUNT NO. 234

TERMS NAME Shell Fuel
RATING ADDRESS
CREDIT LIMIT

DATE 19	ITEMS	FOLIO	/	DEBITS	DATE 19	ITEMS	FOLIO	/	CREDITS
June 7				120 —	June 3				120 —

FIGURE 6.3. LEDGER ACCOUNTS FOR THE ACCOUNTS PAYABLE SUBSIDIARY LEDGER.

SHEET NO. _____						ACCOUNT NO. 235		
TERMS		NAME *N. Y. Light*						
RATING		ADDRESS						
CREDIT LIMIT								

DATE 19	ITEMS	FOLIO	✓	DEBITS	DATE 19	ITEMS	FOLIO	✓	CREDITS
					June 4				88 30

SHEET NO. _____						ACCOUNT NO. 236		
TERMS		NAME *Janitorial Supply*						
RATING		ADDRESS						
CREDIT LIMIT								

DATE 19	ITEMS	FOLIO	✓	DEBITS	DATE 19	ITEMS	FOLIO	✓	CREDITS
					June 3		P J		78 50

FIGURE 6.3. (Continued.)

in the accounts payable column (Figure 6.3). The corresponding credit entries were previously made from the purchase journal. When all the postings have been made from the purchase journal and the cash disbursements journal to our subsidiary accounts payable ledger accounts, we will be able to determine the balance owed to each of our creditors. It is important, then, that the entries to our subsidiary ledger acounts be posted often so that our records are correct at all times.

THE PETTY CASH JOURNAL

The hotel will purchase many items for cash as well as by check. In fact, the accounting office will have a petty cash fund for the items we purchase for cash. These purchases will be for small amounts and will usually be made at the local stores. For example, the chef may need 5 pounds of meat or 2 pounds of cheese to complete a recipe, or we may purchase incidental items at one of the other local stores. When these items are purchased, a receipt is brought to the accounting office and money is given out of the petty cash fund.

The journal used to record these purchases is called the *petty cash journal* and is illustrated in Figure 6.4. Checks are written and recorded in our cash disbursements journal for money placed in the petty cash fund. Usually the check is large enough to bring the fund to a predetermined amount. As the fund is used up, another check is

Petty Cash Journal

Date	Detail	Received	Total disbursed	Food expense	Housekeeping supplies e
June 1		200 —			
1	Groceries for Kitchen		5 50	5 50	
2	Housekeeping Supplies		3 50		3 5
2	Stamps		10 —		
2	Groceries for Kitchen		2 30	2 30	
3	Gas for Truck		6 50		
3	Thumb Tacks		1 50		
3	Groceries for kitchens		1 70	1 70	
4	Gas for car #1		5 50		
5	Paint for lounge		12 30		
6	Mop for housekeeper		6 20		6 2
7		55 —			
	9.50	255 —	55 —	9 50	9 7
	9.70	— 55			
	10.—	200 —			
	1.50				
	12.—	Balance	Credit	Debit	Debit
	12.30	in petty	petty	food	housekeeping
	55 —	cash fund	cash	expense	supplies
			#101	#510	expense
					#531

FIGURE 6.4. PETTY CASH JOURNAL.

written to bring it back to the original amount. We record the receipt
of these amounts in the received column of our petty cash journal,
along with the date of receipt.

Payments from the fund are made when purchase receipts are re-

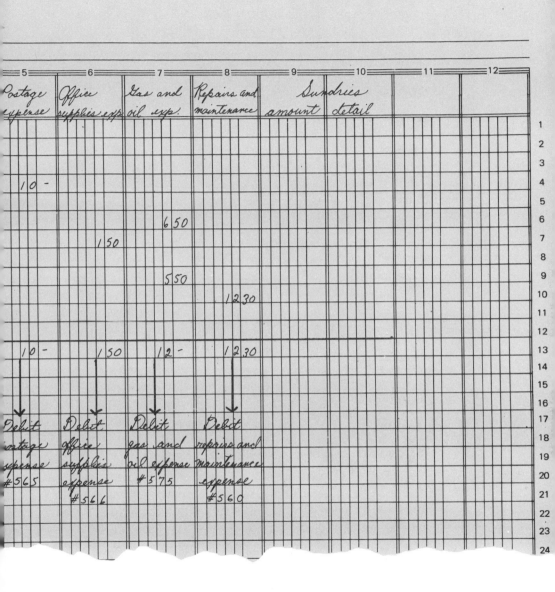

	5	6	7	8	9	10	11	12	
	Postage expense	Office supplies exp	Gas and oil exp.	Repairs and maintenance	Sundries amount	detail			
1									
2									
3									
4	10 –								
5									
6			6 50						
7		1 50							
8									
9			5 50						
10				12 30					
11									
12									
13	10 –	1 50	12 –	12 30					
14									
15									
16									
17	Debit	Debit	Debit	Debit					
18	postage	office	gas and	repairs and					
19	expense	supplies	oil expense	maintenance					
20	#565	expense	#575	expense					
21		#566		#560					
22									
23									
24									

ceived. They are immediately recorded in the detail column. The total amount disbursed is recorded in the next column, and it is apportioned to the appropriate expense or asset. The headings on the petty cash journal will vary considerably from hotel to hotel, but certain headings

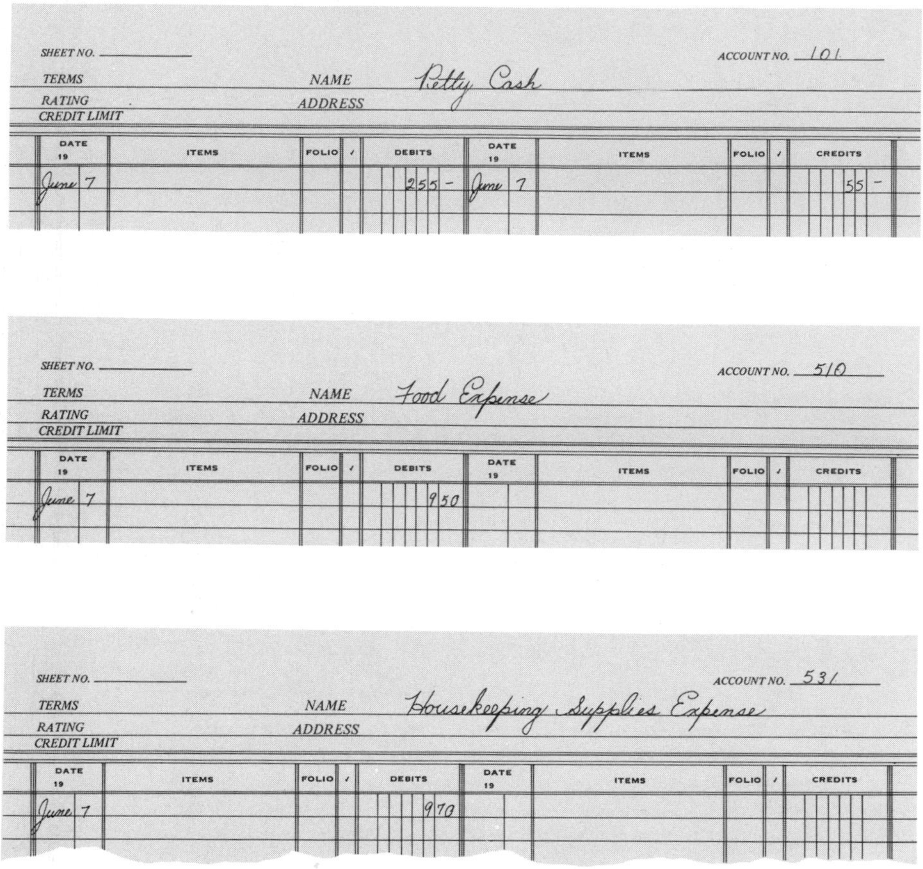

FIGURE 6.5. LEDGER ACCOUNTS FOR PETTY CASH JOURNAL.

will be common to all hotels because certain types of items are purchased for cash frequently by all hotels. Frequently used columns are food expense, housekeeping supplies expense, postage expense, and office supplies expense. A sundries column will be set aside for other purchases not covered by the established columns.

At the end of the month we will balance our journal. The sum of all the expense and asset columns must equal the sum of the total disbursed column. The total disbursed column is subtracted from the total of the received column to determine a balance in the petty cash fund. This bookkeeping figure must agree with the actual cash amount in the fund.

SHEET NO.								ACCOUNT NO. 560		
TERMS			NAME		Repairs and Maintenance Expense					
RATING			ADDRESS							
CREDIT LIMIT										
DATE 19	ITEMS	FOLIO	✓	DEBITS	DATE 19	ITEMS	FOLIO	✓	CREDITS	
June 7				12 30						

SHEET NO.								ACCOUNT NO. 565		
TERMS			NAME		Postage Expense					
RATING			ADDRESS							
CREDIT LIMIT										
DATE 19	ITEMS	FOLIO	✓	DEBITS	DATE 19	ITEMS	FOLIO	✓	CREDITS	
June 7				10 —						

SHEET NO.								ACCOUNT NO. 566		
TERMS			NAME		Office Supplies Expense					
RATING			ADDRESS							
CREDIT LIMIT										
DATE 19	ITEMS	FOLIO	✓	DEBITS	DATE 19	ITEMS	FOLIO	✓	CREDITS	
June 7				1 50						

SHEET NO.								ACCOUNT NO. 575		
TERMS			NAME		Gas and Oil Expense					
RATING			ADDRESS							
CREDIT LIMIT										
DATE 19	ITEMS	FOLIO	✓	DEBITS	DATE 19	ITEMS	FOLIO	✓	CREDITS	
June 7				12 —						

FIGURE 6.5. (Continued.)

The total disbursed column is posted in the general ledger as a credit to petty cash. A debit entry was previously made to that account from the cash disbursements journal. The difference between the debit and credit sides of the petty cash ledger account will also equal the amount in our petty cash fund.

The remaining columns will be posted as debits to the appropriate expense or asset. Figure 6.5 illustrates the postings from our petty cash journal to our ledger accounts.

BALANCING THE ACCOUNTS PAYABLE SUBSIDIARY LEDGER ACCOUNTS

We have referred to the fact that the accounts payable subsidiary ledger accounts must balance with the accounts payable control account, but we have not demonstrated how it is done. We will now explain it.

At the end of each month, the accounts payable subsidiary ledger accounts are added and balances determined for each of them. They are then listed on a schedule and the schedule is added. The figure thus obtained must agree with the amount in our control account. If it does not, we must find the error and correct it before we go any further in the accounting cycle. We have balanced a sample accounts payable subsidiary ledger schedule with the control account in Table 6.1.

Table 6.1. SCHEDULE OF ACCOUNTS PAYABLE

Account number	Name	Amount
231	Allen Meats	$11.00
233	Max Repairs	30.00
235	New York Light	88.30
236	Janitorial Supply	78.50
	Total Accounts Payable	$207.80
	Accounts Payable Control	$207.80

RECAPPING OUR WORK

We have now completed our discussion of the various subsidiary journals. They are used to enable the hotel bookkeepers to handle large numbers of transactions easily and to keep unnecessary clutter from the ledger accounts. Our accounting system has changed from the one developed in Chapter 1. The general journal is now used only for adjusting and closing entries plus any entries that cannot fit in our subsidiary journals. The postings to ledger accounts will come from several journals, but we will not have many postings to each ledger account. Figure 6.6 shows the various debit and credit entries to our ledger accounts.

Each of our journals serves a useful purpose. Each summarizes the transactions for a period of time so that we only make a few postings to a ledger account instead of many, as was the case when we used only a general journal. The summary sales journal provides us with a means for

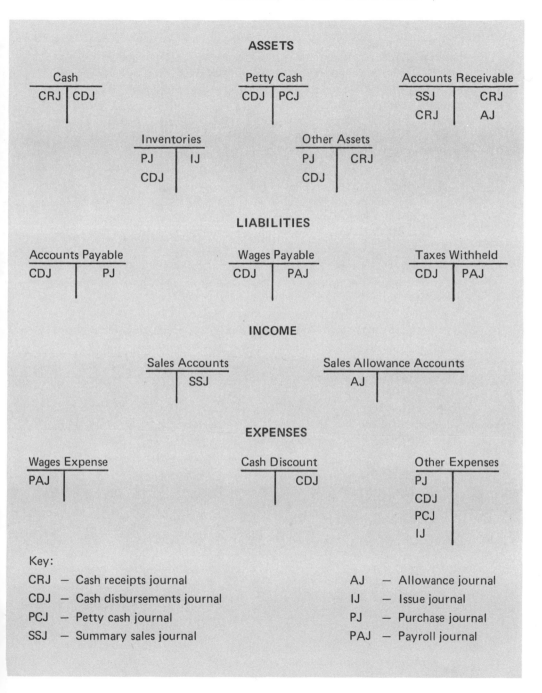

FIGURE 6.6   SOURCES OF DEBITS AND CREDITS TO THE VARIOUS LEDGER ACCOUNTS.

posting totals to our income accounts. The cash receipts and cash disbursements journals provide us with a means of keeping track of cash without unnecessary entries to our ledger account. The purchase journal enables us to post our expenses and inventories to their ledger accounts. The payroll journal gives us a means of determining total payroll. And other journals help us in our objectives of reducing the amount of entries entered in the ledger accounts while enabling us to handle large numbers of transactions. We will now complete the accounting cycle in much the same fashion as we did in Chapter 1.

SUMMARY

The cash disbursements journal is used to record the payment of cash. The journal enables us to credit our cash account and debit liability, expense, or asset accounts.

One of the liability accounts we will debit is accounts payable and another is payroll payable. We can also debit an asset or expense account directly without first entering it into the purchase journal. So we now have two ways of handling purchases. We can first enter purchases into our purchase journal and thereby set them up as accounts payable. When we write a check to pay for the purchases, we enter the information in the cash disbursements journal, crediting cash and debiting accounts payable. The second way is to immediately write a check for purchases and thereby debit the expense account or asset account, without first entering it in the purchase journal.

Small purchases made with cash are recorded in the petty cash journal. The funds for those purchases come from the auditor's bank, which is called the petty cash fund. Each purchase is entered in the petty cash journal and distributed to the appropriate expense account. At the end of the month, the journal is added and totals are posted to appropriate ledger accounts.

QUESTIONS FOR DISCUSSION

1. In what way are the cash discount and sales allowance accounts the same?
2. What kinds of purchases would a hotel normally make that it would write a check for immediately rather than entering it in the purchase journal?
3. Explain how we balance the petty cash fund.
4. Explain the function of each of the major journals we have discussed.

7 | The Departmentalized Work Sheet

After the postings have been made from the various journals to the ledger accounts, they are totaled and a trial balance is taken in the same way as in Chapter 1. The work sheet is completed, financial statements are drawn up, the ledger accounts are prepared for next month, and a post-closing trial balance is taken. We will devote this chapter to the preparation of the work sheet, and we will emphasize adjusting entries and the departmentalized work sheet.

THE TRIAL BALANCE

The ledger accounts are totaled and balances transferred to the work sheet. The work involved in totaling the accounts is much less than in Chapter 1, because we used special journals that summarized the information. Each ledger account will have very few figures to add. And if our trial balance is not correct, it is now much easier to find the mistake. Assuming that we started the month with a correct trial balance, there are just a few possible places our error can be, and the same general procedure for finding mistakes as was explained in Chapter 1 should be used:

1. Readd the debit and credit columns of the trial balance.
2. Verify that all ledger accounts have been entered on the work sheet and that the balances as shown have been properly transferred to the work sheet.
3. Readd all ledger accounts.

4. Recheck postings to be certain equal debits and credits were posted from the journals.

Our subsidiary journals were designed so that each one contained equal debits and credits. If the journals were properly balanced and the totals posted correctly to ledger accounts, they must contain equal debits and credits.

Figure 7.1 shows the new work sheet and columns 1 and 2 show the new trial balance. We have included most of the ledger accounts discussed in the previous chapters, so there are more of them than we worked with in Chapter 1. The asset, liability, and owner's equity accounts contain balances from last month plus additional amounts from the various journals this month. The income and expense account balances are from the subsidiary journals this month. You should be able to determine which journals each of the income and expense accounts came from.

ADJUSTING ENTRIES

You will recall that adjusting entries are planned corrections to our ledger accounts. We make adjusting entries after our trial balance primarily because we do not have the appropriate information for adjusting entries until our trial balance is completed. At the end of a month, and for the first few days of the following month, the accounting personnel are extremely busy. Inventories are being taken of all supplies and merchandise, and all subsidiary journals are being totaled and posted to ledger accounts. Usually it takes two or three days for all inventories to be taken and for the figures to be given to the accounting department. At the same time the inventories are being taken, the accounting department is obtaining a trial balance. The information for some adjusting entries will come to the accounting department at about the same time as our trial balance is completed.

Our purpose in making adjusting entries is to get our ledger accounts as accurate as possible so that, when we draw up our financial statements, they will accurately reflect the state of our business.

Several kinds of adjusting entries will be made. First, we will adjust our inventories to reflect their true values. We have been keeping track of our inventories during the month. Each time supplies and merchandise were put into a storeroom, that information was noted in the purchase journal. Each time supplies and merchandise were taken from a storeroom, that information was also noted in the issue journal. However, our bookkeeping figure will need to be adjusted because food sometimes spoils while in inventory, issues are sometimes made without an issue slip being made out, mistakes are made in pricing when items are issued, and supplies sometimes disappear without anyone's knowledge. We will compare the bookkeeping figure with the actual inventory and adjust our ledger account for the difference in the two figures. Most hotels will accept a difference of about 1 or 2 percent of the value of the issues, but if there is a shortage of more than that amount, an investigation is made into the causes of the shortage. We have adjusted our food inventory, liquor inventory, and housekeeping supplies inventory by debiting the appropriate expense and crediting the inventory. Notice that the amount of the adjustment in each case is about 2 percent of the value of the issues.

Adjustments numbers 4 and 5 are to accounts called prepaid insurance expense and prepaid taxes expense. Explanation is needed as to the nature of these accounts and the reasons for the adjusting entries. A prepaid expense is an expense we expect to incur (but have not incurred yet) and have paid for in advance. It is listed on the balance sheet as an asset, because it has money value to us. As the expense is incurred, we will adjust the prepaid account by means of an adjusting entry. A very good example of this kind of expense is insurance. When we purchase fire insurance, for example, we may pay for the year's policy immediately. We have paid for insurance for a whole year, yet our financial statement covers only one month. It would not be good accounting practice to charge the entire amount of the fire insurance expense to one month's business. Thus, we set it up as a prepaid expense—that is, an expense paid for in advance—and carry it on our books as an asset. The bookkeeping entry would be a debit to prepaid insurance expense and a credit to cash. It has value to us because, if we should decide to cancel the policy, we would receive a refund from the company for the remaining worth of the policy. Each month we will make an adjusting entry and will debit insurance expense and credit prepaid insurance for $\frac{1}{12}$ of the cost of the insurance. At the end of the life of the policy we will have credited prepaid insurance and debited insurance expense for the full amount of the policy's cost. Our books will not show any remaining value in the prepaid insurance ledger account.

The same reasoning is also applied to prepaid taxes. Our property and school taxes are paid for in advance. The amount we pay covers the coming year. Inasmuch as our financial statement covers only one month, we do not want to charge the entire amount of the taxes expense to the business for one month. Instead, we set it up as an asset (debiting prepaid taxes and crediting cash), and each month we debit taxes

		Name	Trial Balance Dr.	Trial Balance Cr.	Adjustments Dr.	Adjustments Cr.	Adjusted Trial Balance Dr.	Adjusted Trial Balance Cr.
1	100	Cash in the bank	2500 -				2500 -	
2	101	Petty cash	200 -				200 -	
3	103	Accounts receivable	1510 67				1510 67	
4	121	Food inventory	2000 -			1) 5 -	1995 -	
5	122	Housekeeping supplies inventory	1000 -			2) 1 -	999 -	
6	123	Liquor inventory	1000 -			3) 1 -	999 -	
7	131	Prepaid insurance expense	1200 -			4) 200 -	1000 -	
8	133	Prepaid taxes expense	2300 -			5) 100 -	2200 -	
9	151	Land	50000 -				50000 -	
10	161	Building	100000 -				100000 -	
11	162	Accumulated depreciation - Bldg		5000 -		6) 150 -		515...
12	171	Furniture and fixtures	35000 -				35000 -	
13	172	Accumulated depreciation F & F		3500 -		6) 50 -		355...
14	181	Linen, china, glass and silver	10000 -				10000 -	
15	201	Accounts payable		3232 80				323...
16	202	Wages payable		100 -	7) 100 -			20...
17	211	Federal Withholding Tax payable		147 10				1...
18	212	Social Security Tax payable		75 15				
19	213	State Withholding Tax payable		26 70				
20	226	Sales Tax payable		152 41				1...
21	251	First mortgage payable		41000 -				410...
22	300	Capital stock		150000 -				1500...
23	301	Retained earnings		2218 90				22...
24	401	Room sales		1938 -				19...
25	402	Room allowances	27 -				27 -	
26	410	Food sales		807 30				8...
27	411	Food allowances	5 -				5 -	
28	421	Liquor sales		336 90				3...
29	430	Telephone sales		51 59				
30	431	Telephone allowances	1 50				1 50	
31	510	Food expense (cost of food)	158 38		1) 5 -		163 38	
32	521	Liquor expense (cost of liquor)	54 -		3) 1 -		55 -	
33	531	Housekeeping supplies expense	45 70		2) 1 -		46 70	
34	541	Telephone expense (cost of sales)	40 -				40 -	
35	550	Wages expense	1266 -		7) 100 -		1366 -	
36	560	Repairs + maintenance expense	67 30				67 30	
37	570	Heat, light and power expense	208 30				208 30	
38			208583 85	208583 85				
39	580	Insurance expense			4) 200 -		200 -	
40	585	Property taxes expense			5) 100 -		100 -	
41	590	Depreciation expense			6) 200 -		200 -	
42					607 -	607 -	208893 85	2088...
43		Net profit (loss)						
44								

FIGURE 7.1.   THE DEPARTMENTALIZED WORK SHEET.

Sheet

Income Statement

	Rooms Dr.	Department Cr.	Food and Beverage Dr.	Dept. Cr.	Telephone Dr.	Department Cr.	General Dr.	Expenses Cr.	Balance Dr.	Sheet Cr.	
1									2500		
2									200		
3									151067		
4									1995 –		
5									999 –		
6									999 –		
7									1000 –		
8									2200 –		
9									50000 –		
10									100000 –		
11										5150 –	
12									35000 –		
13										3550 –	
14									10000 –		
15										323280	
16										200 –	
17										14710	
18										7515	
19										2670	
20										15241	
21										41000 –	
22										150000 –	
23										221890	
24		1938 –									
25	27 –										
26				80430							
27			5 –								
28				33690							
29						5159					
30					150						
31			16338								
32			55 –								
33	4670										
34					40 –						
35	526 –		390 –		100 –		350 –				
36							6730				
37							20830				
38											
39							200 –				
40							100 –				
41							200 –				
42	59970	1938 –	61338	114120	14150	5159	112560				
43	33830		52782			(8991)		(112560)		65061	
44	938 –	1938 –	114120	114120	14150	14150	112560	112560	20640367	20640367	

expense and credit prepaid taxes for $\frac{1}{12}$ of the total tax bill. At the end of the year we will have debited taxes expense for the full amount of our obligation and credited prepaid taxes for its full value.

Adjusting entry number 6 is a debit to depreciation expense and two credits to accumulated depreciation, one to building and the other to furniture and fixtures. Depreciation expense is a recognition of the lessening in value of our assets. It is a legitimate expense to the business and should be deducted from our income to determine profit. For example, an automobile lessens in value each month we own it. After the first year it is only worth about $\frac{2}{3}$ of the purchase price, and after two years it depreciates to about $\frac{1}{2}$ of its original value. We recognize the lessening in value of the automobile by debiting depreciation expense and crediting accumulated depreciation. Notice that no cash is involved in the expense, for we have presumably paid for the asset already. Depreciation is referred to as a noncash expense (as are our other adjusting entries). Other assets that will depreciate include furniture, kitchen equipment, office equipment, and other fixed assets, except land.

One of the difficulties with depreciation is that assets depreciate at different rates. An automobile will depreciate faster than a kitchen stove, and both will depreciate faster than a building. Further, some assets will depreciate equal amounts each year, whereas others will depreciate very rapidly the first few years and then level off for the remainder of their lives. In order to set up a depreciation schedule we must estimate the expected useful life, the depreciation rate, and the residual value of each asset. The federal government also has regulations on depreciation rates, and usually we will follow government guidelines. There are three formulas that are important to us in hotel accounting for determining the amount to be deducted each year as depreciation expense.

The first of the formulas is called straight-line depreciation and is used to determine the rate of depreciation for those assets that lose value in equal amounts each year. Our building is a good example of that kind of asset. The formula for determining straight-line depreciation is

$$\frac{\text{Total cost of asset}}{\text{Number of years of expected life of asset}}$$

A building that cost $30,000 and is expected to last 30 years would be depreciated at an annual rate of $1,000. Each month we would debit depreciation expense and credit accumulated depreciation for $\frac{1}{12}$ of $1,000.

The remaining two methods of depreciation are used for assets that depreciate rapidly during the first years of their lives. Examples of these kinds of assets include automobiles, kitchen equipment, furniture, and accounting machines. The first is called the declining-balance method. The amount of depreciation is determined by applying twice the straight-line rate to the remaining value of the asset each year. For example, the straight-line rate on an automobile lasting five years would be $\frac{1}{5}$ or 20 percent of its purchase price each year. Using the declining-balance method, we would double the rate to 40 percent and depreciate the asset each year by 40 percent of the remaining value of the asset. A car costing $3,500 lasting 5 years would be depreciated as follows:

Table 7.1.   DECLINING-BALANCE DEPRECIATION

Year	Rate (%)	Amount of depreciation	Remaining value at end of year
1	40	$1,400	$2,100
2	40	840	1,260
3	40	504	756
4	40	302	454
5	40	182	272

The remaining portion ($272) would presumably be the residual value of the automobile at the end of five years. The difficulty with the above method is that the asset is never fully depreciated. We are always taking a percentage of a remaining amount. However, it does recognize the fact that a great portion of the value of the car is depreciated during the first couple of years.

The last method of depreciation we will deal with is called the sum-of-the-years'-digits method. It has the advantage of recognizing that an asset depreciates more quickly during its first years of life, but the depreciation rate is more uniform than the declining balance method. The formula can best be explained by illustration.

Using the automobile of our previous example, we first add together the number of years of expected life of the car: $1 + 2 + 3 + 4 + 5 = 15$. We then subtract from the purchase price an estimated residual value. Assume the car's value after 5 years will be $500. The $3,000 remaining will be used in determining the amount to be depreciated each year. In year 1 we will depreciate the car by $\frac{5}{15}$ of $3,000; in year 2 we will depreciate it by $\frac{4}{15}$ of $3,000; in year 3 we will depreciate the car by $\frac{3}{15}$ of $3,000, etc. The depreciation schedule for our automobile would be as follows:

Table 7.2. SUM-OF-THE-YEARS'-DIGITS DEPRECIATION

Year	Rate	Amount of depreciation	Remaining value at end of year
1	5/15	$1,000	$2,500
2	4/15	800	1,700
3	3/15	600	1,100
4	2/15	400	700
5	1/15	200	500

At the end of the fifth year, $500 is shown on the books for our automobile.

The final adjusting entry on our work sheet was a debit to wages expense and a credit to wages payable for $400. That adjusting entry was made to show that there were wages expenses during the period that we did not account for. For example, if payday was on a Friday and the end of the month was the following Monday, we should show that our employees have three days' wages coming to them. And we should increase our wages expense by that amount because they belong in this month's expenses rather than next month's, as would be the case if we did not make the adjusting entry. Quite often there are expenses we should properly recognize during a month, but because no bills had been submitted or because our bookkeeping routine would not cause us to recognize the expense during our normal work, we must recognize the expense in the form of an adjusting entry.

After all adjustments have been recorded on the work sheet, the adjustments column is added, balanced, and the figures are combined with the trial balance in the usual way to arrive at the adjusted trial balance.

THE INCOME STATEMENT PORTION OF THE WORK SHEET

The remainder of the work sheet is considerably different from that in Chapter 1. We have several columns devoted to the income statement rather than only one. The reason for having several columns is to assist us in preparing our financial statements. Our general income statements will contain departmental profits or losses. In order for us to determine departmental income, we will have columns on our work sheet for each of our operating departments. The adjusted trial balance figures are distributed to their appropriate departmental portion of the work sheet. We will not spend much time explaining which particular expenses belong to each department of the hotel because there are far too many to be treated in this text. The *Uniform System of Accounts for Hotels*, published by the American Hotel and Motel Association, lists all the expenses normally found in a hotel and where they belong. However, we can state the general rule which will cover our decisions: If an expense or income can be directly attributed to a department of the hotel, we will charge it to that department. An example is the cost of food. It can be directly attributed to the food and beverage department. The wages of cooks, waiters, and bartenders will also be included as an expense to that department. However, we cannot directly attribute the cost of electricity, repairs to the building, depreciation of the building, the manager's salary, or the cost of operating the company automobile to any specific department, so we will deduct these as general expenses. All expenses and all income will be taken into consideration in determining the final profit or loss for the hotel. Some will be charged to specific departments and others will be deducted on a more general basis.

In our illustration we have assumed that the rooms department includes all the activities of the front office, housekeeping, and bellmen. We have placed the figures for room sales, room allowance, housekeeping supplies expense, and wages expense for the rooms department in that portion of the work sheet. You will recall that our payroll journal listed payroll by department. We did that so we know how much of our total wages expense to attribute to each department of the hotel.

The food and beverage department includes the activities of the kitchen, bar, and dining room. That portion of the work sheet contains food and liquor income, food and liquor allowance, food expense, liquor expense, and the wages expense of those employees in the food and beverage department.

The telephone department portion of the work sheet contains the telephone sales, telephone allowances, cost of sales, and wages attributed to the telephone department.

The remainder of the expenses are placed in the general columns of the work sheet and will be deducted from the departmental profits to arrive at net income.

Each departmental profit is determined, and the total of the profits, less general expenses, is then transferred to the balance sheet in the usual fashion.

THE BALANCE SHEET PORTION OF THE WORK SHEET

All 100, 200, and 300 series account balances are placed in the balance sheet portion of the work sheet. Net profit is added to these figures and a balance is obtained in the same way as in Chapter 1.

SUMMARY

The trial balance using subsidiary journals is obtained in the same way as in Chapter 1. However, it is easier to obtain because we do not have as many postings to our ledger accounts. In the event we make a mistake and do not obtain a trial balance, it is now easier to trace our error.

The trial balance is obtained using the first two columns of our work sheet. Columns 3 and 4 are used for our adjusting entries. Adjusting entries are planned corrections to ledger accounts. We will make adjusting entries to (1) correct our inventory accounts to reflect their true values, (2) adjust the values of our prepaid expenses, (3) adjust the values of our fixed assets, (4) recognize expenses that were not previously recognized, and (5) correct errors that were made during the month.

Depreciation is a noncash adjusting entry. There are three methods of depreciation we are concerned with. Straight-line depreciation is used for those assets that depreciate in equal amounts over the life of the asset. The declining-balance method and the sum-of-the-years'-digits method are used for those assets that depreciate very rapidly during the first years of life of the asset.

The adjusted trial balance is obtained by combining the adjusting entries on our work sheet with the original trial balance. The 100, 200, and 300 series accounts are then transferred to the balance sheet portion of the work sheet. The 400 and 500 series accounts are transferred to the income statement portion of the work sheet, making sure that the expenses for each department are put in the columns for that department. The *Uniform System of Accounts for Hotels,* published by the American Hotel and Motel Association, tells us which expenses go to each department. The general rule is that if an expense can be directly attributed to a department it should be included as an expense of that department. If not, it is deducted as a general or administrative expense.

The work sheet is then completed in the usual manner, and the net profit is transferred to the balance sheet portion of the work sheet.

QUESTIONS FOR DISCUSSION

1. Explain why totaling ledger accounts should be easier when we use special journals than when we use only a general journal.
2. For what purposes is the general journal used now that we have special journals to take care of most of the transactions?
3. Explain which journals each of the income and expense account amounts listed on the work sheet for this chapter came from.
4. Why are adjusting entries sometimes called noncash entries?

5. If we debited insurance expense and credited cash for the full amount of a year's insurance policy instead of setting it up as a prepaid expense, what effect would it have on our first month's income statement? What effect would it have on each of the following month's statements? Would it make any change in a statement drawn up for the entire year?

6. Explain the circumstances for using each of the three methods of depreciation explained in the text.

7. If we did not adjust our wages expense for the amount owed and not paid to our employees, what effect would it have on next month's income statement?

8. Explain why it is important for us to determine our wages expense for each department of the hotel rather than compute it for all employees together.

9. In addition to the extra columns on our new work sheet, are there any other differences in the new and old work sheets?

8 | Completing the Accounting Cycle

The work described in the previous chapter takes place during the first few days of the month. Management and other interested parties are anxious to see the new financial statements and compare the figures with the previous month's results. So, we will prepare these statements as soon as the work sheet is completed, rather than waiting until the books have been closed.

We will devote this chapter to concluding the accounting cycle, and we will emphasize the income statement, balance sheet, and interpretation of the financial statements.

THE NEW INCOME STATEMENT

The information for our new income statement is taken directly from our work sheet. In large hotels with many varied expenses, a separate detailed income statement is drawn up for each department, and the totals are summarized on the general income statement for the hotel. We do not have very many expenses to list for each department, so we will not bother to prepare departmental income statements for any of the departments in our hotel. Instead, we will go directly to the general statement, taking our figures from the work sheet.

Referring to Figure 8.1 let us look at the income statement and determine where the information came from. Net sales for each department is gross sales minus allowances. Gross sales for the rooms department was $1,938 from our work sheet in the last chapter. Room allowances amounted to $27. The difference between the two figures is $1,911 and is placed under net sales. Net sales for food is $804.30 minus $5 allowance or $799.30. Net sales for liquor is the same as gross sales because there were no allowances. Telephone gross sales are $51.59 minus allowance of $1.50, making net sales $50.09.

The next column in our income statement is the cost of sales, and it refers to the cost of merchandise sold to customers. We will probably

Operated Departments	Net sales	Cost of sales	Payroll related
	1	2	3	4
Rooms	1911 -		526
Food	799 30	163 38	390
Beverage	336 90	55 -	
Telephone	50 09	40 -	100
	3097 29	258 38	1016
Gross operating income			
Deductions from income			
Administrative			350
Repairs and maintenance			
Heat, light and power			
			350 -
Gross operating profit			
Taxes			
Insurance			
Profit before depreciation			
Depreciation			
Net profit to retained earnings			

Roger Young's Hotel Income Statement
Period Ending June 31, 19 –

FIGURE 8.1.   INCOME STATEMENT FOR ROGER YOUNG'S HOTEL.

never have any figure entered there for the rooms department because we do not sell goods to anyone renting a room. We sell them only services. The supplies that are used up, such as soap, are not considered cost of a sale, but are considered direct expenses and will be deducted in the column labeled other expenses. However, the costs of food, liquor, and telephone calls are listed, and they are shown on our work sheet as the amounts for food expense, telephone expense, and liquor expense.

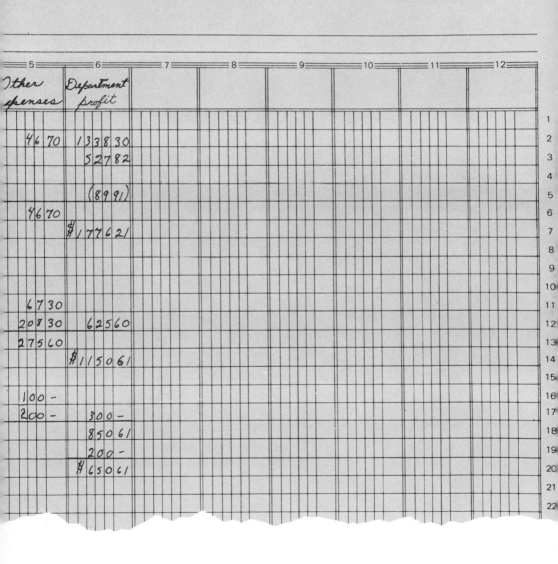

Other expenses	Department profit						
46 70	1338 30						
	527 82						
	(89 91)						
46 70	$1776 21						
67 30							
208 30	625 60						
275 60							
	$1150 61						
100 -							
200 -	300 -						
	850 61						
	200 -						
	$650 61						

The payroll column is used to show the wages expense for each department. There is only one payroll listed for the food and beverage department because some employees work for both departments and it is difficult to allocate part of their wages to each.

The "other expense" column is for the remaining expenses we can directly attribute to each department. As explained in the last chapter, you must refer to the *Uniform System of Accounts for Hotels* to find out which expenses are normally attributed to each department.

The total of all the expense columns is subtracted from the net sales figure to arrive at departmental profits (or losses). They must agree with the profits shown on the work sheet. The departmental profits are added, and the resulting figure is called *gross operating income*. We verify it by subtracting the total expenses of all operating departments from the total sales of all the departments.

We then subtract the expenses listed in the general column of our work sheet from gross operating profit to arrive at net profit. Those general expenses on our work sheet listed as payroll will be put in the payroll column. The net profit shown on our statement must agree with the net profit as shown on our work sheet.

The form of the income statement is specified by the American Hotel and Motel Association, and it is important that it is followed each month. We can compare our statistics each month with past months, and in addition we can compare them with industry averages. If other hotels did not follow the format prescribed by the American Hotel and Motel Association, it would be impossible for us to compare our hotel's statistics with those of other hotels.

THE NEW BALANCE SHEET

The new balance sheet will be drawn up from the figures on our work sheet and will not differ too much from the balance sheets of many other businesses (Figure 8.2). However, there are some terms used that need explanation. Under current assets, we have separate totals for inventories of supplies and inventories of merchandise. Supplies are those assets that are used up in the course of business, such as housekeeping supplies and office supplies. Merchandise comprises those assets that are sold to our customers, such as food, liquor, and cigarettes.

We add together cash, accounts receivable, supplies, merchandise, and prepaid expenses to arrive at total current assets. The total is called current assets because they are (1) cash, (2) can be readily turned into cash, or (3) are expected to be used up during the near

Roger Young's Hotel
Balance Sheet
as of June 30, 19 —

Assets

Current assets:		
Cash in bank	$2,500	
Petty cash	200	$2,700.00
Accounts receivable		1,510.67
Inventories of merchandise:		
Food	1,995	
Liquor	999	2,994.00
Inventories of supplies:		
Housekeeping supplies		999.00
Prepaid expenses		
Insurance	1,000	
Taxes	2,200	3,200.00
Total current assets		$11,403.67
Fixed assets		
Land		50,000.00
Building	100,000	
Less depreciation	5,150	94,850.00
Furniture and Fixtures	35,000	
Less depreciation	3,550	31,450.00
Linen, china, glass		10,000.00
Total fixed assets		186,300.00
Total assets		$197,703.67

Liabilities and stockholder's equity

Current liabilities		
Accounts Payable — Trade	$3,232.80	
Wages Payable	200.00	
Social Security	75.15	
State Withholding Taxes	26.70	
Federal Withholding Taxes	147.10	
Sales Taxes Payable	152.41	
Total Current Liabilities		$ 3,834.16
Long Term Debt		41,000.00
Total Liabilities		$44,834.16
Stockholder's Equity:		
Common Stock — 150,000 shares @ par value $1	150,000.00	
Retained earnings	2,218.90	
Profit for period	650.61	
Total Stockholder's Equity		152,869.51
Total liabilities and stockholders' equity		$197,703.67

FIGURE 8.2. BALANCE SHEET FOR ROGER YOUNG'S HOTEL.

future. They represent our current state of affairs and give us some idea of our ability to get cash in the next accounting period.

Fixed assets on the other hand are long term—that is, we do not expect to turn them into cash or use them up in the near future. We subtract accumulated depreciation from our building account and furniture fixtures account to show the actual book value of each of those assets. We do not depreciate linen, china, or glassware, but we replace these items as they are broken or lost.

The liability and stockholders' equity portion of the balance sheet should be familiar to you. All liabilities are listed, and total liabilities plus owner's equity must equal total assets. The term "current liabilities" refers to all liabilities that will come due within the next financial period. Long-term liabilities are those (such as a mortgage on our property) that will not come due until the next financial period or beyond.

It is customary to list the number of shares of stock on the balance sheet at the original value and add to it the amount of profit retained by the company over the years to determine stockholders' equity. It is important to note that the retained earnings figure is the amount of common stockholders' equity above and beyond the original value of the stock. Therefore, the book asset value of a share of common stock would be determined by adding the value of the stock as shown on the balance sheet to its proportional equity in retained earnings.

INTERPRETING THE FINANCIAL STATEMENTS

The financial statements we have carefully drawn up can only help us if we can interpret them.

The first figures we will look at are from our income statement. We will examine net sales, departmental profits, gross operating income, and net income and compare them with last month's statement and the corresponding month's statement from last year. We will do the same for some of the major expenses such as wages, cost of goods sold, and others. If any of them are considerably different from what we expected, we may want to investigate the causes of the differences. The examination of those figures is our first indication of the trend of our business.

There are several percentages we will want to compute from our income statement. The first is our food cost percentage. It is computed by dividing cost of food by net sales. In our illustration, food cost is $163.38 and net sales is $799.30, approximately 20 percent, a very good food cost percentage. Most hotels will run about a 30 to 35 percent food cost, and those operations that rely on volume to make a profit will usually run a 40 to 45 percent food cost. Liquor cost percentage is computed the same way. We divide total liquor cost by net liquor sales. In our illustration, liquor cost is $55 and liquor sales is $336.90, a 17 percent liquor cost. This is also a very good percentage, as most hotels run about a 23 to 25 percent liquor cost.

Payroll as a percentage of net sales is also computed. Our total payroll is $1,366, and our net sales is $3,097.29, about 44 percent. That percentage is a bit high. Most hotels will operate at about a 35 percent labor cost.

Finally, we will compute the percentage of net income to net sales. Our net income is $650.61 and our net sales is $3,097.29, a 21 percent return on net sales. This figure is indeed extremely good, as industry averages are much less.

Turning to our balance sheet, we will also want to interpret it. We will first look at the individual figures to verify there have been no great changes in any of them from the previous month. We will especially look at the size of our inventories to verify that they are not too large. Also, we will be concerned with the amount of our accounts payable, as a great increase would indicate we have not been paying our bills promptly.

Certain ratios are determined from our balance sheet. The first is called the current ratio, and it is determined by comparing total current assets with total current liabilities. Our total current assets amount to $11,403, and our total current liabilities are $3,864, about a 3 to 1 ratio. The current ratio is an indication of our ability to pay our current obligations. Our ratio is good, because we have ample cash or other assets that we expect to turn into cash to pay our bills.

We will next determine the amount earned on stockholders' equity. The total stockholders' equity was $152,218.90 at the beginning of the financial period. Our earnings this period were $650.61, a little less than .4 percent. At first this figure may seem small, but we must remember that the financial statement covers only one month's business. If we earned the same amount each month, the annual rate would be about 5 percent. In dollar figures, we earned about 5¢ on each share of stock.

There are many other ratios and figures we could determine from the financial statements of our hotel if we were to perform an in-depth study of the business. However, the above ratios and percentages will give us a good indication of how well we are doing. We can then compare our statistics with past months and other hotels in our class. In that way, we can judge whether or not we are performing satisfactorily.

General Journal

	Date	Explanation	Folio	Debit	Credit		
1	June 30	Adjusting Entries					
2							
3		Food expense	510	5 —			
4		food inventory	121		5 —		
5							
6		Housekeeping					
7		supplies expense	531	1 —			
8		Housekeeping					
9		supplies					
10		inventory	122		1 —		
11							
12		Liquor expense	521	1 —			
13		Liquor inventory	123		1 —		
14							
15		Insurance expense	580	200 —			
16		Prepaid insurance	131		200 —		
17							
18		Property taxes					
19		expense	585	100 —			
20		Prepaid taxes					
21		expense	133		100 —		
22							
23		Depreciation expense	590	200 —			
24		Accumulated					
25		depreciation — bldg	162		150 —		
26		Accumulated					
27		depreciation — F&F	172		50 —		
28							
29		Wages expense	550	100 —			
30		Wages payable	202		100 —		
31							
32							

FIGURE 8.3.   JOURNAL ENTRIES FOR CLOSING AND ADJUSTING ENTRIES.

General Journal

Page 2

Date	Explanation	Folio	Debit	Credit		
	Closing Entries					
June 30	Income and expense summary	600	2480 18			
	Room allowance	402		27 -		
	Food allowance	411		5 -		
	Telephone allowance	431		1 50		
	Food expense	510		163 38		
	Liquor expense	521		55 -		
	Housekeeping supplies expense	531		46 70		
	Telephone expense	541		40 -		
	Wages expense	550		1366 -		
	Repairs and maintenance exp.	560		67 30		
	Heat, light and power expense	570		208 30		
	Insurance exp.	580		200 -		
	Property taxes exp.	585		100 -		
	Depreciation exp.	590		200 -		
	Room sales	401	1938 -			
	Food sales	410	804 30			
	Liquor sales	421	336 90			
	Telephone sales	430	51 59			
	Income and expense summary	600		3130 79		
	Income and expense summary	600	650 61			
	Retained earnings	301		650 61		

CLOSING THE BOOKS

The final job of the accountant is to close the books, that is, get them in shape for the new accounting period. You will recall from Chapter 1 that we have two objectives in mind: (1) to transfer our profit to the retained earnings ledger account, and (2) to close out our income and expense accounts so that they read zero. The balances of our asset, liability, and owner's equity accounts will be carried forward to next month.

We have not yet journalized or posted our adjusting entries, so we will do that first. Secondly, we will journalize and post our closing entries. These steps are performed in the same way as in Chapter 1. We debit the income and expense summary account for the amount of all income and expense accounts with debit balances and credit the individual accounts for their amounts. We credit the income and expense summary account for the amount of all income and expense accounts with credit balances and debit the individual accounts with their balances. Finally, we debit the income and expense summary account for the amount of the profit and credit retained earnings for the same amount.

After all postings are made we rule and balance the accounts in the usual fashion. No income and expense accounts will have balances, and the rest of the accounts will have balances and will be carried forward as opening balances for the next month.

Finally we prepare a post-closing trial balance to verify that we properly closed our accounts. The above procedure is illustrated in Figures 8.3, 8.4, and 8.5.

SUMMARY

As soon as the work sheet is completed, the accountant prepares the formal income statement and balance sheet for management. The information for the new financial statements comes from the work sheet.

The income statement contains the departmental profits of each of the departments of the hotel. Departmental profit is determined by subtracting the departmental expenses from the net sales of each department. Net sales is determined by subtracting allowances from gross sales. Departmental profit agrees with the profit shown on the work sheet for each department. Administrative and other expenses are deducted from the total of the departmental profits to arrive at net income.

The new balance sheet is drawn up in the usual fashion. On our new balance sheet we obtain subtotals for current assets, fixed assets, current liabilities, long-term liabilities, and owner's equity. We customarily list the

SHEET NO. ______ ACCOUNT NO. 121

TERMS NAME Food Inventory

RATING ADDRESS

CREDIT LIMIT

DATE 19		ITEMS	FOLIO	✓	DEBITS	DATE 19		ITEMS	FOLIO	✓	CREDITS
June	1	Balance brought fwd		✓	2047 28	June	30		SJ		103 73
	30	2,000	PJ		56 45		30	Adjusting	GJ1		5 -
					2103 73						108 73
							30	Balance carried fwd			1995 -
											2103 73
July	1	Balance brought fwd.			1995 -						

SHEET NO. ______ ACCOUNT NO. 301

TERMS NAME Retained Earnings

RATING ADDRESS

CREDIT LIMIT

DATE 19		ITEMS	FOLIO	✓	DEBITS	DATE 19		ITEMS	FOLIO	✓	CREDITS
						May	31	closing balance			2218 90
						June	30	closing			650 61
						July	1				2869 51

SHEET NO. ______ ACCOUNT NO. 410

TERMS NAME Food Sales

RATING ADDRESS

CREDIT LIMIT

DATE 19		ITEMS	FOLIO	✓	DEBITS	DATE 19		ITEMS	FOLIO	✓	CREDITS
June	30	closing	GJ2		804 30	June	30		SSJ		804 30

SHEET NO. ______ ACCOUNT NO. 510

TERMS NAME Food Expense

RATING ADDRESS

CREDIT LIMIT

DATE 19		ITEMS	FOLIO	✓	DEBITS	DATE 19		ITEMS	FOLIO	✓	CREDITS
June	30		PJ		47	June	30		CDJ		1 85
	30		SJ		103 73						
	30	158.38	PCJ		9 50						
					160 23						
	30	Adjusting	GJ1		5 -		30	closing	GJ2		163 38
					165 23						165 23

SHEET NO. ______ ACCOUNT NO. 600

TERMS NAME Income and Expense Summary

RATING ADDRESS

CREDIT LIMIT

DATE 19		ITEMS	FOLIO	✓	DEBITS	DATE 19		ITEMS	FOLIO	✓	CREDITS
June	30	closing	GJ2		2480 18	June	30	closing	GJ2		3130 79
	30	closing	GJ2		650 61						
					3130 79						

FIGURE 8.4. SELECTED LEDGER ACCOUNTS.

Post Closing Trial Balance

Account no.	Name	Dr.	Cr.
100	Cash in the bank	2500 -	
101	Petty cash	200 -	
103	Accounts receivable	1510 67	
121	Food inventory	1995	
122	Housekeeping supplies inventory	999	
123	Liquor inventory	999	
131	Prepaid insurance expense	1000	
133	Prepaid taxes expense	2200	
151	Land	50000	
161	Building	100000	
162	Accumulated depreciation — building		5150 -
171	Furniture and fixtures	35000	
172	Accumulated depreciation — F & F		3550 -
181	China, linen, glass and silver	10600	
201	Accounts payable		3232 80
202	Wages payable		200 -
211	Federal withholding tax payable		147 10
212	Social security tax payable		75 15
213	State withholding tax payable		26 70
226	Sales tax payable		152 41
251	First mortgage payable		41000 -
300	Capital stock		150000 -
301	Retained earnings		2869 51
		206403 67	206403 67

FIGURE 8.5. POST-CLOSING TRIAL BALANCE.

number of shares of stock at their original value on the balance sheet and add to that the amount of retained earnings to arrive at total owner's equity.

Financial statements are meaningless unless we can interpret them. We first compare the gross figures for this month's income and expenses with those of last month, as well as compare this month's income and expenses with the same month last year. Certain percentages and ratios will also be computed to help us interpret our results. Some of them are food cost percentage, liquor cost percentage, payroll as a percentage of net sales, percentage of net income to net sales, current ratio, and amount earned on stockholders' equity.

The final job of the accountant is to close the books, that is, to get them ready for the next month's entries. Profit is transferred to the retained earnings ledger account, expense and income accounts are closed so that they read zero, all ledger accounts are ruled and balanced, and a post-closing trial balance is prepared.

QUESTIONS FOR DISCUSSION

1. Our income statement shows a departmental profit for the food and beverage department. Why wouldn't we show separate departmental profits for the food department and the beverage department?
2. Explain how we calculate each departmental profit. What is the general rule for determining which expenses are listed as "other expenses" on our income statement?
3. Explain why it is important that hotels use the same form when drawing up their financial statements.
4. Explain the difference between supplies and merchandise.
5. Is there any special significance to the total asset figure at the bottom of the balance sheet? How could we change that figure and not substantially change the business?
6. If there were 1,000 shares of stock originally issued for $100 each and the hotel had retained earnings of $26,000, what is the book value of each share of stock? Would this value have any relationship to its market value if we were to attempt to sell shares to the public?
7. If some food operations have low food cost percentages and some have high food cost percentages, does that necessarily mean that the low food cost operation makes more money than the high food cost operation? Explain.
8. The current ratio is supposed to give us an indication of our ability to pay our current obligations. What evidence is there in the composition of current assets to refute this argument? Can you think of a

ratio that would give us a better indication of our bill-paying ability?

9. Of what significance is the size of our food inventory?

10. Explain why no income or expense account should have a balance after we have posted our closing entries.

9 | Accounting for Small Hotels, Motels, and Restaurants

The accounting system described in the previous seven chapters was designed primarily for larger hotels—those with more than 150 rooms. Most hotels, motels, and restaurants are much smaller and consequently do not need a system that is so complex. Indeed, in the previously described accounting system, we would need a qualified accountant to take care of all the books and prepare the statements for the hotel. The small operation cannot afford to hire a qualified accountant, but instead will hire a bookkeeper or the owner will do the bookkeeping himself. At the end of the financial period, an accounting firm, retained by the operation, will spend a day preparing the formal books. In this chapter we will discuss a few of the various systems used by small hotels, motels, and restaurants to keep their accounting records.

THE CASH AND ACCRUAL SYSTEMS OF ACCOUNTING

The key to understanding the accounting of most small operations is in knowing the distinction between a cash and an accrual system of accounting. The system we have employed to this point is an accrual system—that is, we have recognized all transactions as they have occurred. We have accrued all assets, liabilities, income, and expenses through the accounting period. As sales were made, we debited cash and/or accounts receivable and credited an income account. As we purchased goods, we debited an expense or asset account and credited

155

ROOM NO. _33_

RATE _$ 15_

DATE OF ARRIVAL _5/31_

DATE OF DEPARTURE _6/1_

TRANSFER FROM _____

TRANSFER TO _____

REGISTER CARD NO. _____

M *Mr. James*

New York City

DATE	5/31		6/1														
FORWARD			28	70													
ROOM	15	-															
RESTAURANT	10	-															
``																	
BEVERAGE	2	-															
``																	
TELEPHONE	(35)																
``																	
``																	
VALET																	
LAUNDRY																	
SUNDRIES																	
Tax CASH ADVANCES	1	35															
DR. TRANSFERS																	
TOTAL	28	70															
CREDIT CASH			28	35													
ALLOWANCE				35	*Telephone*												
CR. TRANSFERS																	
BALANCE FORWARD	28	70															

WILLIAM ALLEN & CO., N. Y., STOCK FORM 8100

ALL ACCOUNTS ARE DUE WHEN RENDERED

FIGURE 9.1.   GUEST BILL.

cash or accounts payable. We recognized all transactions as they occurred. Notice, however, that eventually all sales were turned into the receipt of cash and all purchases were turned into the payment of cash, as our guests paid us and as we paid our bills. So, if we had a system where we did not bother to show sales until our guests paid us, or we did not bother to show purchases until we paid our bills, we would eventually come up with the same financial statements and would have simplified our bookkeeping routine.

The cash system of accounting does exactly that. In a pure cash accounting system we do not recognize any income until we receive cash and we do not recognize any expenses until we pay our bills. The key word is "recognize." In an accrual system, we recognize all income and expenses as they occur, and in a pure cash system we recognize income and expenses as we receive or pay cash. The final results should be the same using both systems, because eventually all income is cash and all expenses mean payment of cash. The big advantage of a cash system of accounting is that we can considerably simplify our accounting system. The big disadvantage of a cash system is that we lose a lot of our control.

A PURE CASH SYSTEM OF ACCOUNTING

The pure cash system eliminates the need for many of the subsidiary journals we previously used. We need only a cash receipts journal, cash disbursements journal, and a payroll journal. The cash receipts and cash disbursements journals are illustrated in Figures 9.3 and 9.4. Let's look first at the cash receipts records.

As guests pay their bills, the information is summarized on a front office cash sheet in much the same fashion as before (Figures 9.1 and 9.2). However, the amount paid on each bill is separated to account for that portion of the cash which is a result of room sales, food sales, liquor sales, telephone sales, and sales tax. The totals of the front office cash sheet are then transferred to the cash receipts journal. At the end of the month, the cash receipts journal is totaled, and the information is posted to the ledger accounts crediting the appropriate income accounts and debiting cash. The advances to guests and cash advances collected columns are posted as debits and credits to accounts receivable.

By using this system, we eliminate two of the journals previously used, the summary sales journal and the allowance journal. Any allowances are deducted before payment is made, and the summary sales journal is combined with the cash receipts journal. We may

Front Office
Cash

Account number	Name	Room no.	1 Total received	2 Room	3 Restaurant	4 Bar
524	James	33	28 35	15 -	10 -	2 -
526	Grace	121	29 65	18 -	5 -	
523	Morgan	25	25 10	12 -	6 50	4 -
	Cash sales		52 50		35 -	15 -
	Peters	111	68 55	36 -	24 50	
	Cohen	50	53 50	30 -	12 20	8 5
			257 65	111 -	93 26	29 5

Recap.

Rooms	111.00
Rest.	93.20
Bar	29.50
Tel.	3.75
Cash adv.	8.50
Sales tax	11.70
	257.65
Less Disb.	8.50
Net cash	249.15

FIGURE 9.2.   FRONT OFFICE CASH SHEET — PURE CASH SYSTEM.

Cash Sheet

Date June 1
Cashier B Smith

received.   Cash paid out

5 Telephone	6 Cash advances collected	7 Sales tax	8 Miscellaneous amount	9 detail	10 Name	Acct. no.	11 Room no.	12 Amount	
		1 35			Peters	5 29	1 1 1	3 00	1
	5 50	1 15			Grace	5 26	1 2 1	5 50	2
1 50		1 10							3
									4
		2 50							5
									6
2 00	3 00	3 05							7
25		2 55							8
									9
3 75	8 50	11 70						8 50	10

Cash Receipts

	Date	Total receipts	Rooms	Restaurant (1)	Beverage (2)	Telephone (3)	Cash adva. collected (4)
1	June 1	257.65	111.00	93 20	29 50	3 75	8
2	2	453.60	165.00	120 00	43 50	5 20	2
3	3	326.30	150.00	112 50	35 00	4 60	3
4	4	368.95	170 00	123 20	48 20	6 00	4 2
5							
6		1406.50	596.00	448 90	156 20	19 55	18
7							
8			Credit	Credit	Credit	Credit	Credit
9			room	restaurant	bar	telephone	accoun
10			sales	sales	sales	sales	receivab
11			#410	#410	#421	#931	#103
12							
13		*Balance*					
14							
15		Rooms	596.00				
16		Restaurant	448.90				
17		Beverage	156.20				
18		Telephone	19.55				
19		Cash adv. collected	18.10				
20		Sales tax	62.05				
21		Cigar sales	5.70				
22		Rent	100.00				
23		Total receipts	1406.50				
24		Less disbursements	26.50				
25		Net receipts	1380.00				
26							
27							
28							

FIGURE 9.3. CASH RECEIPTS JOURNAL — PURE CASH SYSTEM.

Journal

	5 Sales tax	6 Front office amount	7 Misc. explanation	8 Other amount	9 Receipts explanation	10 Advances to guests	11 Net receipts	12	
1	11 70					8 50	249 15		
2	17 50			100 —	Store Rent	5 60	448 00		
3	15 50	5 10	Cigar Sales			4 20	322 10		
4	17 35					8 20	360 75		
5									
6	62 05	5 10		100 —		26 50	1380 00		
7									
8	Credit	Credit		Credit		Debit	Debit		
9	sales tax	cigar		rent		accounts	cash		
10	payable	sales		income		receivable	#100		
11	#226	#415		#420		#103			
12									

	Date	Paid to	Check no.	Amount	Food expense	Housekeeping supplies exp
1	June 1	A. B. C. Meat Purveyors	1001	220 30	220 30	
2	1	Mountain Produce	1002	150 00	150 00	
3	2	Bill's Repair Service	1003	52 00		
4	2	State Liquor Store	1004	160 00		
5	3	Janitorial Services Inc.	1005	101 30		101 30
6	4	Jack's Dairy	1006	53 00	53 00	
7	4	Petty cash	1007	21 60	10 50	
8	5	N. Y. Electric	1008	52 30		
9	6	State Liquor Store	1009	42 30		
10	7	Payroll account	1010	430 20		
11				1283 00	433 80	101 30
12						
13				Credit	Debit	Debit
14				cash	food	housekeeping
15				#100	expense	supplies
16					#510	expense
17		Balance				#531
18						
19		Food	433 80			
20		Housekeeping	101 30			
21		Liquor	202 30			
22		Wages	430 20			
23		Repairs & maintenance	52 00			
24		Heat, light & power	52 30			
25		Office supplies	11 10			
26			1283 00			
27						
28						
29						

FIGURE 9.4.   CASH DISBURSEMENTS JOURNAL — PURE CASH SYSTEM.

	5 Liquor expense	6 Wages expense	7 Repairs and maintenance exp.	8 Heat, light and power exp.	9 Office supplies exp.	10 Miscellaneous exp. amount	11 detail	12
1								
2								
3			52 00					
4	160 00							
5								
6								
7					11 10			
8				52 30				
9	42 30							
10		430 20						
11	202 30	430 20	52 00	52 30	11 10			
12								
13	Debit	Debit	Debit	Debit	Debit			
14	liquor	wages	repairs and	Heat, light	office			
15	expense	expense	maintenance	and power	supplies			
16	#521	#550	expense	expense	expense			
17			#560	#570	#582			

also eliminate the restaurant and bar cashier's sheets as well as other departmental sales records.

If we have a number of employees, one journal we will want to keep intact is the payroll journal. Internal Revenue requires us to keep accurate records of our payments to our employees, so we will still want to keep individual payroll records as well as the payroll journal. The journal provides us with a means of verifying the accuracy of our payroll and telling us our liability to Internal Revenue for withholding tax and social security tax. We may or may not post to the ledger accounts from the payroll journal. If we decide not to post to the ledger accounts from the journal, we will have to summarize the information for the various payroll periods when we pay our obligations to Internal Revenue.

The above system is well suited to those hotels, motels, and restaurants with a small number of departments and is particularly good for American plan hotels that charge one rate for room and board and do not offer many additional services. It is also good for small restaurants that sell only food and drink and for those small operations that have cash registers or other machines. The machines will keep totals of cash received for the various departments, and at the end of the day we need only read the totals of the machines and make adjustments to our sales.

Let us turn our attention to the cash disbursements journal illustrated in Figure 9.4 and see what happens to the purchases side of our accounting system. As bills are received, they are filed in a file drawer. Periodically we will go through the file drawer and pull out those bills we wish to pay. As they are approved for payment and a check is issued, the information is written in the cash disbursements journal. The amount paid is distributed to the appropriate expense or asset. At the end of the financial period, the journal is totaled and posted as a debit to expense or asset accounts and a credit to cash. You can see that the amount of expenses for any period of time is directly related to the number of bills we pay. However, in the long run it should not make any difference because all bills will eventually get paid and all expenses will be accounted for.

The petty cash journal will no longer be necessary. The auditor will still maintain his petty cash bank, and he will disburse cash from it. However, he will not need a journal because he will write a check to petty cash periodically for the exact amount he has spent from petty cash. In the cash disbursements journal he will distribute the amount to the expenses involved. Of course, he will save all purchase receipts for future reference.

We have now eliminated three additional journals, the purchase journal, the issue journal, and the petty cash journal.

Merchandise and supplies are considered expenses when we pay the bills so we don't worry about receiving clerk's daily reports or issue slips because we do not keep track of the size of our inventories on a daily basis. We determine their size from a physical inventory at the end of the month, and we adjust our expenses at that time. For example, assume that our food inventory at the end of last month was $3,000 and this month it was $3,100. During last month and this month we paid all the bills for food. We might make an adjusting entry, debiting food inventory and crediting food expense for $100 at the end of the financial period to account for the difference in the physical inventories. In effect we are saying that we put $100 too much in food expense when we paid our bills. We are now adjusting that figure because $100 worth of food purchased last month was not used but is still in inventory.

Advantages and Disadvantages

The obvious advantage to a pure cash system of accounting is its simplicity. Only three subsidiary journals are used. We do not have to hire an expensive accountant to take care of our bookkeeping, but need only a qualified bookkeeper. Further, small hotels and restaurants do not need a complicated set of books. Management can exercise personal supervision over events; and they know the significant details of their business because of their close personal contact with it.

On the other hand, there are at least two big disadvantages to the pure cash system of accounting. In the short run it is not as accurate as the accrual system. Revenue is not recorded until money is received, and expenses are not taken into consideration until bills are paid. Thus, our daily, weekly, and monthly figures may or may not reflect the true condition of our business. Of course, over a period of several months, it should be as accurate as the accrual system.

Second, the cash system of accounting does not provide controls that are as effective as the accrual system. You will recall that our accrual system was set up so that all revenue was debited to accounts receivable or cash. The total revenue for each department was verified by the night auditor, and all sales were either charged to guest bills or collected in cash. The total accounts receivable always agreed with the amount remaining on our transcript of guest ledger. Using the cash system, it is possible for guest bills to be unpaid or lost without our knowing it. On the expense side, we cannot keep track of our daily expenses because we no longer have a purchase or issue journal; it is possible for shortages to exist in our storeroom without immediate corrective action being taken.

Thus, in order for a pure cash system of accounting to be effective,

FIGURE 9.5. SUMMARY TRANSCRIPT — ACCRUAL SYSTEM.

Summary Transcript

TRANSCRIPT OF GUEST LEDGER

DATE *June* 197__

SHEET NO. ____

ROOM NUMBER	NO. PERS.	CARD NUMBER	~~NAME~~ *Date*	BALANCE AT BEGINNING OF DAY DEBIT	BALANCE AT BEGINNING OF DAY CREDIT	ROOM	TAX	REST.	BEVERAGES	PHONE	TELEG.	LAUNDRY	VALET	BAGG.		CASH DISBR.	TRANS.	TOTAL CHARGES	CREDITS CASH	CREDITS ALLOW.	CREDITS TRANS	BALANCE AT END OF DAY DEBIT	BALANCE AT END OF DAY CREDIT
			June 1	992 50		320 –	35 50	250 80	76 30	10 60						5 30		698 50	423 40	5 20		1262 40	
			2	1262 40		300 –	32 –	241 50	70 00	11 20						6 20	26 30	687 20	533 80		26 30	1389 50	
			3	1389 50		280 –	25 50	203 60	65 40	9 30						5 80		589 60	822 70	10 00		1146 40	
			4	1146 40		260 –	26 50	200 10	60 30	10 00						1 00		557 90	630 40			1073 90	
			5	1063 90		300 –	35 00	314 00	86 20	8 50						10 50		754 20	420 50	6 00		1401 60	
			6	1401 60		350 –	38 50	306 50	100 50	15 30						6 00	11 50	828 30	935 20		11 50	1283 20	
			7	1283 20		230 –	23 50	132 20	121 60	6 30						8 30		521 90	660 00			1145 10	
				8549 50		2040 –	216 50	1648 70	580 30	71 20						43 10	37 80	4637 60	4426 00	21 20	37 80	8702 10	
																		– 37 80					
						Credit Room Sales #401	Credit Tax Payable #226	Credit Rest Sales #410	Credit Bar Sales #421	Credit Telephone Sales #430								4599 80		Posted as Debits To Allow. Accounts and Credit To Accounts Receivable			
																		– 43 10					
																		4556 70					
																		Debit Accounts Receivable #103					
			Proof	2040 –																			
				216 50																			
				1648 70																			
				580 30																			
				71 20																			
				43 10																			
				37 80																			
			TOTAL CHARGES	4637 60																			
			Opening balance	8549 50																			
			Plus total charges	+ 4637 60																			
				13187 10																			
			Minus credits	4485 00																			
			Balance	8702 10																			

Balance	
Room	2040 –
Tax	216 50
Rest	1648 70
Bar	580 30
Phone	71 20
	4556.70

(4556.70 = 4556 70 Debit Accounts Receivable #103)

Notes:

1. Dr and Cr. transfer columns must be equal.
2. Cash column equals guest receipts column in cash receipts journal.
3. Cash disbursements column equals advanced to guests column in cash receipts journal.

management must exercise close personal control over income and expenses. The system is fine for small businesses and family operations, but does not work very successfully in larger hotels.

AN ACCRUAL ACCOUNTING SYSTEM FOR SMALL OPERATIONS

It is possible to establish an accrual system for small operations that does not require the extensive bookkeeping of the larger operations yet provides management with adequate controls.

The accrual system for small hotels relies heavily on the transcript of guest ledger. You will recall that the transcript of guest ledger was not an integral part of our bookkeeping system but was primarily used to provide control over front office activities. We verified that all guest charges were accurately posted to guest bills and all bills were arithmetically correct. However, the transcript does provide us with essentially the same information that goes into our summary sales journal; so as long as we have that information, why not use it to good advantage? We can eliminate the need for a summary sales journal and an allowance journal if we consider our transcript a journal.

We post the totals of each daily transcript sheet to a summary transcript sheet. At the end of the month, we add the summary transcript and post the totals to our ledger accounts. Figure 9.5 illustrates this procedure. The total of the summary transcript rooms column is posted as a credit to room sales, the total of the restaurant column is posted as a credit to restaurant sales, and the remainder of the sales columns posted as credits to their respective sales accounts. The total of all sales is posted as a debit to accounts receivable. Notice that all sales are considered charge sales, because all sales are included on our transcript totals.

The information for our transcript comes from our guest bills, so we may or many not have separate departmental revenue sheets. For example, in an American plan hotel where room and board are all one rate, we should not need a restaurant cashier's sheet, because we will not have any cash sales. And in a smaller hotel, we may not feel the need for a restaurant cashier's sheet because management may exercise close personal control over the restaurant. The night auditor would verify restaurant sales by adding the guest checks from the restaurant and verifying that total with the total on his transcript. Thus, the transcript takes the place of the summary sales journal.

However, it will not take the place of the cash receipts journal because we must have a means of recording all cash as it is received, not

	Date	Day	1 Guest receipts	2 Sundries amount	3 Sundries detail	4 Total receipts
1	June 1	Monday	423 40			423 40
2	2	Tuesday	533 80	100 -	Store Rent	633 80
3	3	Wednesday	822 70			822 70
4	4	Thursday	630 40	5000 00	Bank Loan	5630 40
5	5	Friday	420 50			420 50
6	6	Saturday	935 20			935 20
7	7	Sunday	660 00			660 00
8			4426 00	5100 00		9526 00
9						
10			Credit	Credit rent income		
11			accounts	for $100		
12			receivable	Credit loans payable		
13			#103	for $5,000		
14						
15						
16				Balance		
17			4426 00			
18			5100 00			
19			9526 00			
20						
21						
22						

FIGURE 9.6. CASH RECEIPTS JOURNAL — ACCRUAL SYSTEM.

just that cash from guests paying their bills. It will still be necessary for us to maintain a cashier's sheet because we must use it for verification of the cashier's drawer and as a subsidiary record for our cash receipts journal. The cash receipts journal (Figure 9.6) will be simpler, however, because all sales are considered charge sales. We will not need a column for cash sales. The guest receipts column is posted at a credit to accounts receivable, the sundries column entries are posted as credits to the specific asset, liability or income account, the advances to guests is posted as a debit to accounts receivable, and the net receipts column posted as a debit to cash.

Journal

5 Advances to guests	6 Net receipts	7	8	9	10	11	12	
5 30	4 18 10							1
6 20	6 27 60							2
5 80	8 16 90							3
1 00	5 6 29 40							4
10 50	4 10 00							5
6 00	9 29 20							6
8 30	6 51 70							7
43 10	9 48 2 90							8
								9
Debit Accounts receivable #103	Debit Cash #100							10
								11
								12
								13
								14
								15
								16
	9 48 2 90							17
	43 10							18
	9 52 6 00							19
								20
								21
								22

We may or may not use an allowance journal. If we have a large number of allowances, it will be necessary to use an allowance journal. However, most small hotels do not have very many allowances, so the total of the allowance column on the summary transcript is analyzed at the end of the month and posted as debits to their allowance accounts. The total of the allowance column would also be posted as a credit to accounts receivable.

On the expense side of our accounting system, we can also simplify our procedures. Most smaller hotels do not wish to keep daily records of inventories, and they do not wish to have all the paper work that

Purchase

Date	Creditor	Amount	1 Food expense	2 Housekeeping supplies exp	3 Liquor expense	4
June 1	Swift Inc.	130 00	130 00			
1	Bill's Repair Service	23 30				
2	Morgan's Plumbing Service	63 20				
2	Quality Purveyors	78 50	78 50			
2	Housekeeper's Inc.	130 00		130 00		
3	United Office Products	23 60				
4	N. Y. State Electric	130 00				
5	State Liquor Store	155 30			155 30	
6	Murray Fuel	250 00				
6	Swift Inc.	128 70	128 70			
		1112 60	337 20	130 00	155 30	
		Credit accounts payable #201	Debit food expense #510	Debit housekeeping supplies expense #531	Debit liquor expense #521	
	Balance					
	Food	337.20				
	Housekeeping	130.00				
	Liquor	155.30				
	Repairs	86.50				
	Heat, light, power	380.00				
	Office supplies	23.60				
		1112.60				

FIGURE 9.7.   PURCHASE JOURNAL — ACCRUAL SYSTEM.

Journal

	Repairs and maintenance expense	Heat, light and power	Office supplies exp	Miscellaneous amount	detail				
	5	6	7	8	9	10	11	12	
1									
2	23 30								
3	63 20								
4									
5									
6			23 60						
7		130 00							
8									
9		250 00							
10									
11	86 50	380 00	23 60						
12									
13	Debit	Debit	Debit						
14	repairs and	heat, light	office						
15	maintenance	and power	supplies						
16	expense	expense	expense						
17	#560	#570	#582						

was necessary in our old system. As supplies and merchandise are needed, authorized persons are allowed to enter the storerooms and take what is necessary without bothering to make out an issue slip. We will not use an issue journal, but we will still need a purchase journal. We will not bother with a receiving clerk's daily report, but will initial all invoices as goods arrive, indicating that all goods are received in proper order. The invoices are entered in our purchase journal in the usual manner, but we will not distribute them to inventory and expense accounts as we previously did. We will enter them directly in expense

Cash Disbursements
Credits

	Date	Paid to	Check number	Amount	Cash discount	Accounts payable
1	June 2	Swift Inc.	1001	127 40	2 60	130 00
2	2	Bill's Repairs	1002	23 30		23 30
3	4	Morgan Plumbing	1003	63 20		63 20
4	5	Quality Purveyors	1004	77 00	1 50	78 50
5	5	Housekeepers Inc.	1005	130 00		130 00
6	7	Payroll Account	1006	785 30		
7	8	Macey's Furniture	1007	750 00		
8	9	United Office Products	1008	23 60		23 60
9				1979 80	4 10	448 60
10						
11				Credit	Credit	Debit
12				cash	food	accounts
13				#100	expense	payable
14					#510	#201
15						
16		Balance				
17				448 60		
18		1979.80		785 30		
19		4.10		750 00		
20		1983.90		1983 90		
21						
22						
23						

FIGURE 9.8. CASH DISBURSEMENTS JOURNAL — ACCRUAL SYSTEM.

accounts (see Figure 9.7). These accounts will be adjusted on the basis of a physical inventory at the end of the month as shown earlier in this chapter. For example, if our inventory of food at the beginning of the month was $3,000, and during the month we purchased $5,000 worth of food, and at the end of the month our inventory was $3,500, we would have to make an adjusting entry at the end of the month. We would debit food inventory and credit food expense for $500 to show that $500 worth of food was added to inventory out of this month's purchases and that the same amount of food previously recognized as

Journal

Debits

	5	6	7	8	9	10	11	12	
	Payroll payable	Sundries amount	detail						
1									
2									
3									
4									
5									
6	785 30								
7		750	New Chairs						
8									
9	785 30	750							
10									
11	Debit	Debit							
12	payroll	furniture							
13	payable	and							
14	#302	fixtures							
15		#171							
16									
17									
18									
19									
20									
21									
22									

Cash Receipts and Credits

	Date	Day	1 Food sales	2 Bar sales	3 Sales tax	4 Accounts receivable
1	June 1	Monday	435 00	110 00	26 10	
2	2	Tuesday	370 00	95 00	22 30	21 50
3	3	Wednesday	410 50	100 20	20 50	17 80
4	4	Thursday	320 30	65 50	19 20	36 40
5	5	Friday	500 60	120 30	31 10	23 50
6	6	Saturday	625 20	185 60	40 60	1 05 0
7	7	Sunday	265 40	46 20	10 20	
8			2927 00	722 80	170 00	109 70
9						
10			Credit	Credit	Credit	Credit
11			food	bar	sales tax	accounts
12			sales	sales	payable	receivable
13			#410	#421	#226	#103
14		Balance				
15						
16		Food	2927 00			
17		Bar	722 80			
18		Tax	170 00			
19		Accounts receivable	109 70			
20		cigar	24 80			
21			3954 30			
22						
23		Cash	3667 80			
24		Accounts receivable	286 50			
25			3954 30			
26						
27						
28						

FIGURE 9.9.   CASH RECEIPTS AND SALES JOURNAL FOR A RESTAURANT.

Sales Journal

Debits

5	**6**	**7**	**8**	**9**	**10**	**11**	**12**		
Sundries		Cash	Accounts						
amount	detail		receivable						
		571 10							1
		472 40	36 40						2
6 30	cigars	531 80	23 50						3
		409 00	32 40						4
		601 70	73 80						5
18 50	cigars	760 00	120 40						6
		321 80							7
24 80		3667 80	286 50						8
									9
Credit		Debit	Debit						10
cigar		cash	accounts						11
sales		#100	receivable						12
#431			#103						13
									14

food expense was not used at all but remains in inventory. In T-account fashion, the entries would show as follows:

Food inventory			Food expense	
$3,000			$5,000	$500
500				

There is also another way of handling the same type of transaction. If we assume that all purchases of merchandise and supplies go into inventory, we would determine our expenses on the basis of a physical inventory at the end of the month. In our previous illustration, we would debit food inventory for the full amount of our $5,000 worth of food purchased during the month and adjust it at the end of the month by crediting food inventory and debiting food expense for $4,500. In T-account fashion it would show as follows:

Food inventory			Food expense	
$3,000	$4,500		$4,500	
$5,000				

The formula for determining the amount to be debited to food expense and credited to food inventory is as follows:

Opening inventory + purchases = total available
Total available — closing inventory = cost of goods sold

In the above example, the opening inventory is $3,000. Our purchases during the month were $5,000, and our ending inventory was $3,500. $3,000 + $5,000 = $8,000, the amount of food available for sale. $8,000 — $3,500 = $4,500, the amount of our food expense for the month.

Our accrual system for smaller operations, then, eliminates many subsidiary records that were necessary before. We do not need many of the departmental revenue records, nor do we need any receiving or issuing records except the invoice that accompanies the goods. In addition, we have eliminated several of the journals: the summary sales journal, the allowance journal, and the issue journal, and we may also eliminate the petty cash journal if we like. We do, however, need a cash disbursements journal, as illustrated in Figure 9.8.

ACCOUNTING FOR RESTAURANTS

A restaurant needs a simpler accounting system than a hotel. The expense side of accounting will not change. A purchase journal and a cash disbursements journal will be needed if an accrual system is to be used. A cash disbursements journal will be needed if a pure cash system is used.

On the income side, only a combination sales and cash receipts journal will be necessary. Sales are summarized by adding all the individual

Holiday Restaurant Income Statement For the Period June 1 to June 7	1	2	3	4
Net Sales:				
Food	2927 00			
Bar	722 80			
Other income	24 80			
Total sales		$ 3674 60		
Less Expenses:				
Food	690 00			
Liquor	151 20			
Wages	1235 70			
Repairs and maintenance	53 20			
Supplies for Office	22 60			
Heat, Light and Power	110 00			
Taxes	120 00			
Insurance	50 00			
Depreciation	235 00			
Total expenses		2667 70		
Net Profit		1006 90		

FIGURE 9.10. INCOME STATEMENT FOR A RESTAURANT.

sales slips (guest checks) and verifying them with the total of the cash register, if one is used. If a cash register is not used, it is wise to use a restaurant cashier's sheet. The information is transferred to the combination sales and cash receipts journal illustrated in Figure 9.9. Columns are provided for credits to restaurant sales, bar sales, sundries, and accounts receivable. Corresponding debits are to cash and accounts receivable. The credit accounts receivable column is used for that money received by the restaurant for previous charges; and the debit accounts receivable column is for current charges to accounts.

A payroll journal of the usual form is necessary, as is a cash disbursements journal. Totals of the journals are posted to ledger accounts at the end of the month in the normal fashion, and the accounting cycle is completed. Inventories are taken at the end of the month and our asset accounts are adjusted.

The income statement will be of the standard variety, rather than departmentalized as in a hotel. Figure 9.10 illustrates it.

SUMMARY

The accounting system described in the previous chapters was an accrual system—that is, all income and expenses were recognized as they occurred. However, the accrual system requires a complicated set of books that are not necessary for a small operation.

Most small hotels and restaurants use a form of the cash system of accounting. They only recognize transactions when they receive cash or pay bills. Since all income is eventually turned into cash and all bills incurred are eventually paid with cash, the cash system of accounting is satisfactory for most small operations. The advantages of the cash system of accounting are simplified bookkeeping procedures and the need for only a bookkeeper instead of a qualified accountant to take care of the books. The disadvantages of the cash system of accounting are short-term inaccuracies and lack of control.

When a hotel or restaurant uses a pure cash system of accounting, only three subsidiary journals are necessary—a cash receipts journal, a cash disbursements journal, and a payroll journal. Allowances are deducted before income is recognized; the summary sales journal, the purchase journal, the issue journal, and the petty cash journal are not necessary.

Some hotels use a combination of the cash and accrual systems of accounting. Some recognize income on a cash basis and expenses on an accrual basis. Others recognize income on an accrual basis and expenses on a cash basis. Some smaller hotels use the transcript to take the place of the summary sales journal, and thus recognize income on an accrual basis.

QUESTIONS FOR DISCUSSION

1. Distinguish between a cash system and an accrual system of accounting.
2. Why would a small owner-managed hotel or restaurant prefer to use a cash system?
3. Why does the author state that the cash system of accounting requires the manager to keep a close personal watch on all phases of the business?
4. Explain why a cash system of accounting will not give accurate day-to-day results of business transactions.
5. Explain how the accrual system of accounting for small hotels eliminates much of the paper work necessary in a larger operation.
6. Is the accrual system of accounting for small hotels really a true accrual system? Where do we not recognize all transactions as they occur?
7. Explain why a petty cash journal is not necessary in a smaller hotel.
8. Why are we able to combine the cash receipts journal and the sales journal in a restaurant operation, but unable to do so in a hotel when an accrual system is used?

10 | Reports to Management

One of the tasks of the accounting department personnel is to prepare daily reports of the activities of the business so that management can be kept up to date. These reports will vary from hotel to hotel because different managers desire different information. Some managers want the full information each day about all phases of the operation, and others only wish to have the essential information about sales, room occupancy, food costs, and bank balance. We will examine some daily reports in this chapter.

DAILY REPORT OF INCOME

Of primary importance to the manager is the income of the hotel, because he knows he must maintain it if he is to make a profit. Figure 10.1 illustrates a form which can be used for the daily report of income to management. These forms vary, and we have chosen one which contains the information most managers want.

The first section of the report deals with the sources of income and shows all the income of the various departments of the hotel. The income auditor provides us with the information taken from the summary sales journal, cash receipts journal, transcript of guest ledger, cash disbursements journal, allowance journal, and checkbook. The sales information is put on the report for the day's sales and compared with the sales of each department for the same day last year. It is significant to note that the comparison may or may not be meaningful.

Daily Report of Income

DAY Wednesday   WEATHER Sunny—Warm   DATE June 15, 19 —

Department	Sales today	To date this month	Same day last year	To date this month last year
Rooms	$ 560.00	$ 7,935.00	$ 535.00	$ 7,640.00
Food	320.30	4,365.20	318.40	4,210.00
Beverage	185.50	2,565.60	192.60	2,832.40
Telephone	23.20	342.60	10.10	302.40
Other		475.40	25.30	432.80
Total Sales	$1,089.00	$15,683.80	$1,081.40	$15,427.80

ROOMS STATISTICS

	Today	This month to date	Same day last year	This month to date last year
Number of rooms available	60	845	61	842
Number of rooms occupied	40	563	36	520
Number of guests	47	693	42	672
Average rate per occupied room	$14.00	$14.09	$14.09	$14.69
Average rate per guest	$11.92	$11.45	$12.74	$11.37
Percent of occupancy	67%	67%	59%	62%

CASH REPORT

Todays receipts:		Bank balance:	
Cash sales	$ 235.10	Yesterday	$3,622.50
Accounts receivable	1,321.00	Deposit	1,551.60
Other		Total	5,174.11
Less advances	(4.50)	Less withdrawals	1,840.00
Net receipts	$1,551.60	Balance today	$3,334.11

FOOD INCOME BY MEAL

Meal	Number of covers	Total income	Average per cover
Breakfast	43	$ 59.50	$1.26
Lunch	34	75.60	2.22
Dinner	40	185.20	4.63
Total	117	$320.30	XXXX

FIGURE 10.1. DAILY REPORT OF INCOME.

We are comparing the closest day to the same date last year. But many major holidays fall on the same *date* rather than the same day. When one takes into consideration that fact, the weather for the day, and other special considerations such as economic conditions, strikes that may close public transportation, etc., it is difficult to interpret the comparison with any degree of meaning.

The comparison of the income this month with the income this month last year should be more meaningful to us. It gives us a good idea of the trend of our business. For example, if our total sales for rooms are off 10 percent for the year as compared with last year and this month indicates no change in the trend, we could conclude that we are in financial trouble, and we may want to take extra measures to increase business or decrease costs.

The second section of the report deals with the specific rooms statistics, and we obtain this information from the night auditor. "Rooms available" means that number of rooms which were available for sale. Many times we must put rooms out of order because they are being repainted, redecorated, or used by staff. When a room is out of order, we normally do not include it in those rooms available for sale. "Rooms occupied" comes directly from the transcript and shows the total number of rooms with paying guests. The total rooms occupied plus those vacant equals the total available for sale.

To arrive at the average rate per occupied room, we divide the total room revenue by the number of rooms occupied. That figure will give us an indication of how much revenue we are getting out of a typical room. It is easily influenced by (1) the number of persons in each room and (2) whether we are selling the high- or low-priced rooms. Since we charge more for a room rented to two or more persons than one rented to a single person, we can expect our average rate per occupied room to go up if lots of families or couples are staying in the hotel. Also, if we are able to sell our high-priced rooms, our average rate will go up.

The average rate per guest is total room revenue divided by the total number of guests. That figure will be higher if we have lots of singles and lower if the rooms are fully occupied. The reason for this is that the rate goes up only slightly for each additional person we put in a room.

The percentage of occupancy is perhaps the most important statistic because it tells us how many of our available rooms we were able to rent. To arrive at that figure we divide the total number of rooms occupied by the total number available for occupancy. Most commercial hotels must run at 65 to 70 percent occupancy in order to break even.

June 15   19

Daily Steward Report to Manager
FOOD

	This Date			Month to Date		
Total Stock on Hand this A. M.	$ 1 87 65 0	XXX		$ 1 80 5 55	XXX	
Add: Purchases	1 97 25	XXX		1 40 3 00	XXX	
Total	$ 2 07 3 75	XXX		3 20 8 55	XXX	
Less: Issues	8 6 40	XXX		1 22 1 20	XXX	
Total Stock on Hand this P. M.	$ 1 98 7 35	XXX	$	1 98 7 35	XXX	

	PURCHASES				ISSUES				
	This Date		Month to Date		This Date	%	Month to Date		%
Meat	$ 1 25 80	$	6 01 20	$	33 70		$ 5 10 50		
Poultry and Game			1 30 50		1 0 20		1 32 60		
Fish			1 63 80				1 56 30		
Vegetables	5 6 20		1 70 60		1 1 20		1 63 80		
Fruit			4 6 30		5 00		4 5 50		
Butter			4 0 20		5 50		3 5 05		
Eggs			5 0 20		6 40		4 5 80		
Milk and Cream	1 5 25		5 5 70		5 50		4 5 05		
Groceries			1 0 2 50		8 90		6 5 80		
Ice Cream			4 2 00				2 0 80		
TOTAL	$ 1 97 25	$	1 40 3 00	$	8 6 40		$ 1 22 1 20		

RECEIPTS

	This Date			Month to Date		
Dining Room	$ 3 20 30	100%	$	4 36 5 20	100%	
Coffee Shop	—			—		
Banquets	—			—		
TOTAL	$ 3 20 30		$	4 36 5 20		

SUMMARY

	This Date			Month to Date		
TOTAL RECEIPTS	$ 3 20 30	100.%	$	4 36 5 20	100.%	
TOTAL ISSUES	8 6 40	27%		1 22 1 20	28%	
GROSS PROFIT	2 33 90	73%		3 14 4 00	72%	

Remarks:

Steward

Hotel

Wm. Allen & Co., N. Y. Stock Form 7099

FIGURE 10.2.   DAILY STEWARD REPORT TO MANAGER — FOOD.

Motels usually require less occupancy because they have lower fixed overhead. Seasonal resort hotels usually must have 80 to 90 percent occupancy during the season to break even.

The third section of the report deals with the cash position and tells

DAILY STEWARD REPORT TO MANAGER
BEVERAGE

	This date	Month to date
Total stock on hand this AM	$1,188.10	$1,494.70
Add: Purchases	119.70	524.50
Total	1,307.80	1,919.20
Less: Issues	55.50	666.90
Total Stock on hand this PM	1,252.30	1,252.30

	PURCHASES		ISSUES			
	This date	Month to date	This date	%	Month to date	%
Whiskey, Rye, & Bourbon		114.80	10.50		123.70	
Scotch & Irish	65.80	104.30	12.30		192.40	
Gin	45.20	164.20	9.70		103.40	
Rums		35.80			35.80	
Brandies		15.20			40.70	
Cordials		8.20			32.40	
Vermouths		7.40			8.20	
Total liquor	111.00	449.90	32.50	59%	536.60	80%
Wines — sparkling			7.50	14%	32.40	5%
Wines — still			6.40	11%	32.20	5%
Beer and ale	8.70	62.30	7.60	13%	55.20	9%
Soft drinks		12.30	1.50	3%	10.50	1%
Total	119.70	524.50	55.50	100%	666.90	100%

Summary	This date	%	Month to date	%
Total income	$185.50	100%	$2,565.60	100%
Total issues	55.50	30%	666.90	26%
Gross profit	130.00	70%	1,898.70	74%

FIGURE 10.3.   DAILY STEWARD REPORT TO MANAGER — BEVERAGES.

the manager the amount of cash received, the amount paid out, the current bank balance, and the amount owed by guests. This information is very important to the manager because he knows that certain expenses will be coming up—payroll taxes, etc.—and he always wants to have sufficient cash on hand to take care of them. It will give him a good idea how fast he will be able to pay his bills.

The final section of the report shows the breakdown of food income by meals and dining room. The total income for breakfast, lunch, and dinner for each of the dining rooms will give management a good indication of how much of his food income is derived from each room and each meal. He can compare these figures to last year or last month to get a trend upon which to make judgments. The average cover is usually included, to give management an indication of how much each guest is eating. For example, if dinner income is down, it may be because the number of people served is less, or it may be because they are eating less expensive items.

DAILY REPORT OF EXPENSES

Managers differ in the information they desire about the daily expenses of the business. However, there are two reports that many managers require, and they provide management with the essential information about two of the largest expenses in the hotel, food and liquor. These reports are the steward's daily food report to manager (Figure 10.2) and the steward's daily beverage report to manager (Figure 10.3). Significantly, the information contained in them can be provided only if the hotel is operating with a full set of journals or is keeping a separate record of the purchases and issues from food and liquor storerooms.

We will discuss the food report first. It can be filled out by the steward or a member of the accounting department. Sometimes the food cost accountant is charged with the responsibility of preparing the report. The first part tells the manager the balance of the food inventory. The size of the inventory at the beginning of the day plus what was purchased less what was issued gives the amount on hand at the end of the day. The inventory balance is important to the manager because he does not want it to get too large. If it does, he will necessarily have too much money tied up in inventory, and there is a good possibility food will spoil before it can be used. The breakdown of the purchases and issues is given in the second section and shows the manager exactly which kinds of food the steward is purchasing as well as which kinds of food are being used.

The third section is provided so that the last section can be determined. You will recall that the manager already has the receipts information from the daily report of income. The final section provides the manager with the most important information in the report, that is, the gross profit on sales and the daily food cost percentage. The daily food cost percentage is his best guide to the efficiency of the kitchen. Each menu is priced using a predetermined food cost percentage. Some restaurants are high food cost operations and rely on volume to make a profit; others will be low food cost operations. A high food cost percentage usually means low menu prices, and a low food cost percentage usually means high menu prices. Other things being equal, the operation with the lower prices usually gets more customers than the higher priced one. (The rule does not hold true in all cases, because some restaurants with high prices have exceptionally good food and many people are willing to pay those prices.) In any event, the food cost percentage is predetermined, and the manager will judge the efficiency of the kitchen on how well the chef is able to maintain his food cost percentage.

The beverage report tells the manager essentially the same information about beverage costs. The first section deals with total stock on hand. The size of the inventory is not as critical as in the food department, because it is necessary that large supplies of wines and liquor be on hand. A well-stocked bar is essential to a successful liquor business. Of course, the manager does not want to unnecessarily tie up money in inventory, so he will be concerned that it does not grow too large.

The second section gives the manager the information about the purchases and issues of liquor, wine, beer, and soft drinks. That information helps the manager determine what his clientele are drinking. He will be interested in the percentage of liquor issues to total issues. Normally, beer sales are not as profitable as liquor sales, and he will watch that trend of business. Wine sales are considered additional income, so he will be very interested in the issues of wine.

The last section gives the manager the essential information about his liquor costs. As with food, liquor costs are predetermined, and management will want to be certain that it is maintained. The liquor cost percentage is usually about 24 to 28 percent in a typical hotel bar.

SUMMARY

An important part of an accountant's job is preparing daily reports to management so that managers can be kept up to date on the financial activities of the business. These reports are essential if sound business judgments are to be made. Managers each require different information.

Some want only the basic information about sales, room occupancy, food costs, and bank balance; others want more complete information on a daily basis.

The daily report of income is management's key barometer of business. The report compares the revenue for each day with the same day last month, and compares the total revenue for each month with the total revenue last month up to that particular day. The report also gives the manager other essential information, such as the average rate per occupied room, percentage of occupancy, average rate per guest, the amount of cash in the hotel's bank account, and the breakdown of food income by meal.

The steward's daily report provides the manager with essential information about the expenses of the business. It gives him information concerning inventory balance, issues for the day, and food and liquor cost percentages for the day.

QUESTIONS FOR DISCUSSION

1. Explain the significance of (a) average rate per occupied room, (b) average rate per guest, and (c) percentage of occupancy.
2. Can the percentage of occupancy be changed by putting additional rooms out of order? Explain your answer.
3. The author has stated that the manager wants to be sure sufficient cash is on hand to pay current obligations. Can you determine why the manager would not want too much cash in his checking account for a long period of time?
4. Why would a seasonal hotel need a higher percentage of occupancy than a year-round hotel to break even?
5. Explain why a high food cost restaurant usually has lower menu prices than a low food cost restaurant for the same item.
6. If the food cost percentage is higher than we predetermined, explain some possible reasons for it.
7. If our liquor cost percentage is lower than we predetermined, explain some possible reasons for it.
8. If you noticed that your beer sales were rising and your liquor and wines sales were decreasing, what might you conclude about (a) your clientele, (b) your prices, and (c) the quality of your drinks.

Index